The Dream Team

The Dream Team

The Rise and Fall of DreamWorks:
Lessons from the New Hollywood

Daniel M. Kimmel

Ivan R. Dee   Chicago

THE DREAM TEAM. Copyright © 2006 by Daniel M. Kimmel. All rights reserved, including the right to reproduce this book or portions thereof in any form. For information, address: Ivan R. Dee, Publisher, 1332 North Halsted Street, Chicago 60622. Manufactured in the United States of America and printed on acid-free paper.

www.ivanrdee.com

The paperback edition of this book carries the ISBN 1-56663-752-X.

Library of Congress Cataloging-in-Publication Data:
Kimmel, Daniel M.
   The dream team : the rise and fall of DreamWorks : lessons from the New Hollywood / Daniel M. Kimmel.
     p. cm.
   Includes bibliographical references and index.
   ISBN-13: 978-1-56663-654-4 (cloth : alk. paper)
   ISBN-10: 1-56663-654-X (cloth : alk. paper)
   1. DreamWorks Pictures—History. I. Title.
PN1999.D74K56 2006
384'.80979494—dc22
                                                                2006013915

Dedicated to the next generation,
our family's collective dream for the future:
Amanda Kimmel
Liza MacEntee
Stefanie Leibowitz
Michael Leibowitz

Acknowledgments

AFTER COMPLETING the story of the creation of the FOX broadcast network (*The Fourth Network*), I turned my attention to the present book, the story of DreamWorks. I was gratified when one of the people whose path I crossed on this journey said it was exactly the right subject. Those two start-ups—one a success and the other a failed dream—summed up the story of the American entertainment industry in the last quarter-century.

In similar fashion to my research for the FOX story, I made several attempts to secure the cooperation of Dream-Works in this project, all of which came to naught. Jeffrey Katzenberg's office responded politely to several entreaties but, in the end, he would not talk. Attempts to approach the company through its New York and Los Angeles offices eventually led to terse e-mails from chief publicist Terry Press insisting that I provide her with documentation about what I was doing. Repeated inquiries asking what, exactly, she was looking for got no response. Promised interviews from people involved in film production failed to happen, and some simply said no up front, saving themselves and the author from wasting time.

The reasons for this lack of access are numerous, including the well-known privacy concerns of the principals. David Geffen, for example, cooperated with *Wall Street Journal* reporter Tom King on the biography *The Operator* and then withdrew his support in the midst of the project. Steven Spielberg rarely grants interviews unless he has a new movie to promote. But these attitudes don't explain why even ex-employees were reluctant to speak. Why would TV executives be so much more open than film executives?

Television is a wide-open field, with numerous broadcast and cable channels and networks and production companies. Some people leave one job and go into a related field or a new start-up. The movie world, particularly at the major studio level, is much smaller. Your rival today may be your employer tomorrow, and the fewer opportunities for an executive who is out of work—like, say, Jeffrey Katzenberg in 1994 when he was let go from Disney—means that people are afraid to burn bridges they may later need. Add to that the fact that DreamWorks remains inevitably associated with Steven Spielberg who, for good or ill, is one of the most powerful filmmakers in history. Everyone wants to be in business with him, and deals have been consummated on the notion that Spielberg *might* make a film at the studio in the future. Clearly this was not a man to risk offending by cooperating with a history of his company without his official imprimatur.

Even if Spielberg or Katzenberg should someday write their memoirs, we may never get to see a truly inside story of the short life of DreamWorks. While there are undoubtedly some wonderful anecdotes that have yet to be collected in print, I have made every effort to see that *The Dream Team* is as complete a history of the business as possible.

I want to begin by thanking those who did speak with me, provided me with leads or documentation, or in any way helped collect another piece of the puzzle. While I remain responsible for how those pieces are put together here, I am grateful to Tim Doyle, Bert Fields, Esq., Ruth Galanter, Wilma J. Hunter, Bill Jarosz, Marc Lumer, James Robert Parish, Bruce Robertson, Nat Segaloff, John J. Shaeffer, Esq., Ken Solomon, Ed Symkus, Mike Ventrella, and Gary K. Wolf. Thanks also to the staffs at the Boston Public Library, the Brookline Public Library, and the Mugar Library at Boston University.

I am also grateful to my agent, Alison Picard, who can't always bend the publishing world to my will but never gives up trying. Finally, thanks to my editor and publisher Ivan Dee for his support and comments, but more particularly for not blanching when I told him in September 2005 that I would not be turning in the manuscript due that month because DreamWorks was in the process of negotiating its sale. Without a moment's hesitation he agreed that of course we should let Messrs. Spielberg, Katzenberg, and Geffen write the end of our story. That we did and that they did, and this book is the result.

D. M. K.

Brookline, Massachusetts
July 2006

Contents

The Dream Team

Prologue:
Happy Anniversary

OCTOBER 2004.

It was an unusual ad, even by the standards of the Hollywood trade papers. To people not in the entertainment industry, the typical ads in *Variety* and *Hollywood Reporter* seem strange. The one- or two-page promotions trumpeting a new movie aren't trying to impress readers with its stars but with its box office grosses. A studio noting that its new release has crossed the $100 million benchmark is par for the course. Sometimes the studio executives are disappointed that an expensive movie made "only" $100 million. They'll take out the ad anyway.

Some of the advertisements are intended to do little more than convey "make nice" messages. If someone in the business is named man or woman of the year by a charity or industry organization, friends and colleagues will take out full-page ads congratulating the honoree, perhaps noting some connection with the person, assuming it exists. If not, they'll still place the ad, just to be on the safe side. Today's stranger might be tomorrow's employer, business partner, or even chief executive officer. Almost anything is an excuse for such back-patting. It might be something as simple as one of the trades doing a special section honoring someone's twenty-fifth year in show business or the two-hundredth episode of a TV series. These sections are done with the knowledge that everyone will feel obligated to buy an ad lest they appear to be snubbing the center of attention.

This particular ad, though, was different. It ran for four pages in black and white, and three of those pages were given over almost entirely to hundreds upon hundreds of names in tiny type. Some people must surely have needed a magnifying glass to peruse the lists. Three names were easy to read, even though they were handwritten. They were at the bottom of the fourth page: Steven, Jeffrey, David. A small photo of the three of them appeared on the first page, but nowhere were their last names mentioned. They didn't have to be. The audience for this ad could easily supply the names themselves: Spielberg, Katzenberg, Geffen.

The ad was addressed to the employees of DreamWorks, which on October 12, 2004, celebrated the tenth anniversary of its founding. Ostensibly addressed to the "Dream-Workers," it was really a message to the rest of Hollywood. That message was, "We're still here."

The trio of founders made a point of publicly thanking the company's employees, all of whom were listed on the middle two pages of the spread. There top executives like film chiefs Walter Parkes, Laurie MacDonald, and Michael DeLuca, or ace publicist Terry Press, appeared in the same miniscule font as the anonymous bean counters and secretaries unknown to anyone outside of co-workers, family, and friends. It was just the sort of touch that defined DreamWorks from the beginning, the notion that it was a different kind of studio. The DreamWorkers were told,

"[S]ince any successful business is built by the people who make it happen every day, we set out to recruit a group of people who would be excited by the road less traveled. We needed dreamers and entrepreneurs, people who were unafraid to take creative risks, people who would have the courage to look forward and the strength to withstand naysayers. . . . [W]e remain, as always, amazed by all you have accomplished over the past ten years and grateful for your unflagging loyalty and commitment."

The fourth page was a different sort of list, with a slightly larger type face. It was a "special thanks to all the filmmakers who contributed their talents to make our dream a reality." Mimi Leder, director of the first DreamWorks release, *The Peacemaker*, was on the list. Actor Kevin Spacey, actress Annette Bening, writer Alan Ball, and director Sam Mendes, the principals behind the Oscar-winning *American Beauty*, were there. Mike Myers, Cameron Diaz, Eddie Murphy, and John Lithgow, the starring voice actors for the animated smash hit *Shrek*, were on the list. From the epic blockbuster *Gladiator* were such names as star Russell Crowe, director Ridley Scott, and even the late actor Oliver Reed, who had died in 1999 during production and presumably wouldn't be seeing the ad. If you were a player in Hollywood and your name wasn't on the list, you would still have to be impressed by the company you might be keeping at DreamWorks.

Yet just fourteen months after this ad appeared, the DreamWorks story was over. By then virtually every part of the company had been sold off or shut down. All that was left was the animation unit, now a separate and publicly traded company, and those parts involved in the production and distribution of live-action film and TV. This latter package, subject to months of negotiations, had finally been purchased by Paramount Pictures. The DreamWorks logo—the Tom Sawyer–like boy dropping his fishing line off a crescent moon—would continue, and for the foreseeable future the unit would continue as a self-contained production entity within Paramount. But the dream that Steven Spielberg, Jeffrey Katzenberg, and David Geffen had announced in the fall of 1994—a wide-ranging entertainment company that would produce films, TV shows, music, and interactive games while setting new standards for the coming century—was done.

What went wrong? Investigating the DreamWorks story, one finds many clues but no definitive answer. Certainly there were successes, including the first feature animation unit that not only successfully challenged the Disney behemoth for box office success but, with *Shrek*, gained bragging rights by winning the first Oscar in the new category for feature-length cartoons. In addition, for a few years the Oscar race for best picture had been a showdown between DreamWorks and Miramax, the art film distributor founded by Bob and Harvey Weinstein and acquired by Disney.

Yet there were also indications of a diffuse chain of command and a lack of vision that, in the end, produced a great many films that looked like they could have come from any other studio. Grand projects, announced with much fanfare, were later quietly abandoned, notably a state-of-the-art high-tech production facility that was never built.

As DreamWorks shrank, the company insisted this was all part of the plan, that Steven, Jeffrey, and David were firmly in control, and that no, of course they wouldn't be selling the company. By mid-2005 that tune had changed, especially in the wake of the disastrous release of *The Island*, a science-fiction blockbuster from director Michael Bay that was derided as the worst film of the summer, if not the year. By that point DreamWorks was talking with Universal about a buyout, thought to be a good fit not only because Spielberg's Amblin' Entertainment (his still operative production company) was housed there but because a good portion of DreamWorks was still located in its "temporary" offices at Universal City. When *The Island* tanked, speculation followed that General Electric, Universal's parent company, might be having second thoughts about a purchase of DreamWorks.

For most of its short life, DreamWorks existed in a bubble. Its successes were rightly hailed, its failures noted, but few doubted the assured success of the enterprise. There would be questions over the years, but the founders of the company were three of the most successful men in show business. Given their track records, how could they possibly fail?

1

Dramatis Personae

IN THE BEGINNING there was the troika. They couldn't do it alone—not financially, and certainly not operationally—but as far as the world was concerned DreamWorks was made up of three people. There were superstar director and producer Steven Spielberg, music industry titan David Geffen, and former Disney executive Jeffrey Katzenberg. Studios had been formed before, and many production companies had come and gone, but one would have to go back to the founding of United Artists in 1919 to find anything launched in Hollywood with the impact of DreamWorks. United Artists had been created by four of the biggest names in the then-nascent film industry: pioneering director D. W. Griffith, movie stars Douglas Fairbanks and Mary Pickford, and legendary comedy star and filmmaker Charlie Chaplin. DreamWorks would do it with only three, none of whom had performed in front of the camera in any role other than as themselves.

First and foremost, at least in the public mind, was Spielberg. He wasn't necessarily first among equals in the troika, since Geffen and Katzenberg had their own impressive and formidable resumés, but they were behind-the-scenes guys whereas Spielberg was a filmmaker who had become a brand name. This put him in a highly elite group. Someone like Martin Scorsese might be respected by knowledgeable critics and moviegoers, but Spielberg's name on a movie conveyed information to the general public even when they knew nothing else about the film. There were very few filmmakers who could compare with that reputation. Alfred Hitchcock, the "Master of Suspense," certainly had been a brand name. Cecil B. DeMille, perhaps. Frank Capra in the thirties, Francis Ford Coppola in the seventies, Woody Allen in the eighties. Yet Spielberg was not simply a director but also a producer of other people's films. It was his name, not the director's, that caught the filmgoer's eye on such projects as *Poltergeist*, *Back to the Future*, *An American Tail*, *Gremlins*, and TV miniseries like *Taken* and *Into the West*. There was simply no question that from the outset, merely by his presence, Steven Spielberg was one of DreamWorks's most valuable assets.

Steven Spielberg has been manipulating audiences almost from the moment of his birth. According to his biographer Joseph McBride, he was born in Cincinnati on December 18, 1946, a year earlier than has sometimes been reported. His early love for movies is part of his story. He made his first film, the epic amateur effort *Firelight*, when he was a high school junior. It had its "world premiere" at a movie theater in Phoenix. By his early twenties Spielberg had a contract at Universal, breaking into an industry at a time when it was still dominated by the giants of the past. But Universal executive Sidney Sheinberg took a liking to a short film Spielberg had made called *Amblin'* and brought him aboard.

As young Spielberg began directing his first professional effort in February 1969—a segment of the NBC supernatural television series *Night Gallery*—such veterans as Alfred Hitchcock, Howard Hawks, William Wyler, Billy Wilder, and John Huston were still active. These were men who could trace their careers back to the 1930s or even earlier. Indeed, the draw for Spielberg's piece was not the tyro director but its aging star, Joan Crawford, in a rare television appearance. That was about to change. The phenomenal success of *Easy Rider* that summer put all of Hollywood on a search for films and filmmakers able to appeal to younger viewers. Suddenly experience was out and youth was in. As a result, Martin Scorsese, Brian DePalma, George Lucas, and Steven Spielberg would all benefit from early career breaks.

Spielberg toiled on various TV series produced on the Universal lot—*Marcus Welby, M.D.*, *Columbo*, *Owen Marshall: Counselor at Law*, and *The Name of the Game*. He was learning his craft. His big chance came with an opportunity to do an ABC Movie of the Week. The 1971 *Duel* allowed Spielberg to flex his muscles. The story, by Richard Matheson, was about a man driving down a California highway who realizes that—for no discernible reason—the truck on the road behind him plans to stalk him to the death. Dennis Weaver played the man—named Mann—and we learn little of him and virtually nothing of the anonymous truck driver. It was the law of the jungle, kill or be killed, transplanted to the open road. *Duel* was a notable success for a television film and even became a hit in Europe as a theatrical release. The powers-that-be knew this was a kid to watch.

Spielberg went on to make his professional bow as a big-screen filmmaker with *The Sugarland Express*, and then in 1975 permanently changed the movie business with the release of *Jaws*. For anyone who went to the movies that summer, *Jaws* was a phenomenon. As he would do many times over in the years to come, Spielberg cannily crafted a film that tapped into the mood of the time and rode it to box office success. Although there were solid performances in the film—the leads were Richard Dreyfuss, Robert Shaw, and Roy Scheider—what people talked about was the shark. It was obvious that Spielberg knew how to shoot and put together film for maximum impact. The first shark attack, of a young woman alone in the water, was horrifying precisely because he wouldn't let us see what was happening. He orchestrated the tension to perfection, in the process catapulting himself to the front ranks of Hollywood.

Two years later he was back with a science-fiction hit, *Close Encounters of the Third Kind*, which might have been the film of the year but for the fact that his friend George Lucas had released *Star Wars* a few months earlier. Lucas's film had the greater impact, but *Close Encounters* was a big success in its own right, and Spielberg was on top of the world. Then, with *1941*, it all came tumbling down.

1941 was a disaster. It cost an estimated $35 million and made less than that in its initial U.S. run. By contrast, *Jaws* cost roughly $12 million and made some $260 million at the domestic box office. *1941* was overproduced and self-indulgent. The movie, a comedy about a feared Japanese attack on the California coast, opened with a gag based on *Jaws*. Spielberg hired Susan Backlinie, who had played the victim of the first shark attack, to go out swimming again. John Williams's signature *Jaws* theme suggested a new shark attack, but instead the woman was menaced by a Japanese submarine. As Spielberg biographer McBride notes, "While mildly amusing, the scene went on far too long, and it was a bit early for Spielberg to begin paying homage to his own movies."

The film was shot over eight months and had a huge cast, including Toshiro Mifune, Robert Stack, Ned Beatty, and Christopher Lee, but it was led by *Saturday Night Live* bad boy John Belushi. Belushi would later show himself to be a capable actor in *Continental Divide* and *Neighbors* before his untimely death from a drug overdose in 1982. Here, though, he was cast as a pilot nicknamed "Wild Bill" and was let loose as if he were still playing Bluto from his earlier film hit *Animal House*. Audiences stayed away in droves, as the Hollywood joke put it, and though *1941* eventually made its money back in worldwide release and ancillary sales, the bloom was off the Spielberg rose.

Spielberg's return, ironically, was through his friend Lucas, who produced *Raiders of the Lost Ark* with Spielberg directing Harrison Ford, who had come to attention in Lucas's *American Graffiti* and *Star Wars*. This was to be Spielberg's penance, working as a director for someone known to keep a sharp eye on the budget, proving he could make a successful film without losing control. In that he succeeded. *Raiders*, distributed by Paramount Pictures, was the studio's biggest hit to date, and Spielberg received an Oscar nomination (his second after the one for *Close Encounters*), even if reviews were not always kind. "It says nothing of consequence," lamented veteran critic Archer Winsten in the *New York Post*, while Pauline Kael suggested that producer Lucas was "hooked on the crap of his childhood."

Kael might have been talking about Spielberg as well, for now that he was bankable again he set out on what would be his tribute to suburbia, *E.T.: The Extra-Terrestrial*. This 1982 blockbuster eclipsed Spielberg's early career. Not only was *1941* forgiven and forgotten but Spielberg was now hailed as the creator of the most successful movie of all time, a spot *E.T.* would hold until well into the next decade. After *E.T.*, Spielberg's place in the Hollywood firmament was secure. He could now direct and produce as he saw fit, picking his projects as he pleased. There would be flops and misfires, of course. There would also be the scandal surrounding the omnibus *Twilight Zone: The Movie*, where Vic Morrow and two child actors died during the shooting of John Landis's segment. (Spielberg was one of the film's producers and also directed one of the four stories.) There would also be the disappointment of being shut out at the Oscars for his "grown-up" film adaptation of *The Color Purple*. But Spielberg was an industry force now. Almost as a consolation prize, Spielberg was given the Irving G. Thalberg Award in 1987 by the Motion Picture Academy, an award voted by the Academy's board of governors for distinction as a *producer*. He was not the first director to be so honored. Alfred Hitchcock had never won a directing Oscar and was given the Thalberg in 1968 as his distinguished career was winding down with his final films. Spielberg might well have suspected that his honor was the Academy's way of saying he would never make the sort of important but middlebrow movie the Academy favored for its top prizes.

At last, in 1993, Spielberg showed everyone he could do it all. He turned out another amusement-park ride of a film, *Jurassic Park*, which featured eye-popping computer-animated dinosaurs and replicated his earlier successes. Then, having failed to win respect as a "serious" filmmaker with *The Color Purple* and *Empire of the Sun*, he finally dared Hollywood to snub him when he released *Schindler's List*. Of course they could not. Although it still showed him more of an expert craftsman than a sophisticated story-teller, his harrowing Holocaust film—shot in black and white as if to emphasize how the showman wasn't focusing on the box office—won critical kudos and worldwide box office acclaim. (While it couldn't crack the $100 million mark in the United States, it earned more than $300 million in total world ticket sales.)

Now Spielberg truly had it all professionally: wealth, power, public acclaim, and the acknowledged respect of his peers when he won the Oscar for Best Director for *Schindler's List*, and the film was named Best Picture. (It would win in seven of the film's twelve nominated categories.) He was not yet fifty. What was there to do next?

David Geffen was born February 21, 1943, in Brooklyn. His first big break in the entertainment industry came when he got a job in the mailroom of the New York office of the William Morris Agency, one of the most important talent organizations in the business. He got the interview by claiming to be a cousin of music producer Phil Spector. He had a connection to Spector all right, but a very tenuous one: Geffen's brother Mitchell was married to a woman whose girlfriend was, at the time, married to Spector. After dropping out of college, Geffen had used this connection to visit the studio in California where Spector worked. According to Geffen's biographer Tom King, the music producer treated Geffen shabbily. Using Spector to get the job at William Morris was a neat bit of getting even. More problematic was Geffen's false claim to have been awarded a degree from UCLA. Another trainee had been fired for lying on his application, and Geffen dreaded that his bosses would check on him.

He started showing up in the mailroom early to snatch the letter from UCLA, which he knew would say he had never attended. He then arranged for his brother, a Los Angeles attorney, to send a letter confirming that David had a degree in theater arts. Geffen kept the job, but he had created a needless problem for himself: in 1964 a college degree was not required for a mailroom job at William Morris.

Geffen began working his way up the ladder and by 1968 was hired away by Ashley Famous Agency, the same firm that had rejected him four years earlier for having no degree and a spotty employment record. Geffen was now making a name for himself in the music industry, building up a client roster at Ashley that included Laura Nyro and Joni Mitchell. One of his legendary deals was hooking up the trio of Crosby, Stills, and Nash with Neil Young, then booking the newly minted quartet into what would become the 1969 concert at Woodstock.

In 1971 Geffen founded Asylum Records, a label that soon introduced the world to the Eagles and Jackson Browne. Established artists like Linda Ronstadt and Bob Dylan also recorded for Asylum, making it such a hot property that it was acquired by Warner Communications the following year. Warners already had a part ownership in Asylum and now wanted to pay Geffen for the rest. Geffen asked for an outrageous sum—$7 million—and to his surprise Warners agreed, paying him some $2 million up front and giving him the balance in Warners stock, making Geffen one of the largest shareholders of the company. He also became a salaried employee of Warners at $150,000 per year.

By the mid-seventies Geffen had money and power. He was not only active in the music business but had begun dabbling in film. He was known to the public, if at all, as the entertainment executive who was having a well-publicized romance with Cher (then in the middle of her breakup with Sonny Bono). He also developed a love/hate relationship with studio executive Barry Diller, then at Paramount. Through him he met Diller's young assistant, twenty-four-year-old Jeffrey Katzenberg. Katzenberg did a lot of Diller's scut work, and Geffen got to see just how efficient Katzenberg could be when he arranged for Geffen and Diller to be hustled through customs in New York on a return trip from Europe.

"That was the quickest ride through customs I ever had," Geffen said in amazement, seeing an eight-years-younger version of himself in Katzenberg.

At this point Geffen had a long overdue showdown with Ted Ashley, chairman and CEO of Warner Bros. Pictures. The details are less important than the fact that Geffen lost. He was kicked out of Warners and given a ceremonial job as "executive assistant" to Steve Ross, chairman of Warner Communications. Ross wouldn't release Geffen from the remaining three years of his employment contract even though Geffen had no interest in such a bogus job. Geffen soon had more serious things to worry about when he was diagnosed with bladder cancer. Upon surgery the tumor was declared to be malignant, though it had not spread. It had been a horrible scare, but Geffen survived. Indeed, Geffen later found that the tumor had not been malignant after all. Such misdiagnoses were not unheard of, but dealing with what seemed to be a life-threatening medical crisis kept Geffen away from the music business for several years.

He returned in 1979 when his Warners contract at last expired. Soon he was back in the music business as head of a new label, Geffen Records. In spite of the fact that he had had such a bad experience with Warners, he accepted financing from Warner Bros. Records, in large part because he continued to feel comfortable with its chief, Mo Ostin. Geffen Records would become a joint venture with Warners, with the entertainment conglomerate assuming much of the financial risk in return for half the new company's assets.

Geffen was soon on a roll. His first artist was Donna Summer, about to become the queen of disco. His next acquisition was the John Lennon / Yoko Ono *Double Fantasy* album, released just days before Lennon's tragic murder. Soon the Geffen roster included such recording artists as Elton John, Neil Young, and—a little later on—Guns N' Roses. He then branched out into theater production (*Cats*, *Dreamgirls*) as well as the movies (*Risky Business*, *Personal Best*, *Little Shop of Horrors*).

Geffen was moving in new circles now. He became friendly with film director Steven Spielberg and suggested to him that Spielberg start putting some of his money into an art collection. Spielberg's first acquisition was a painting by the Belgian surrealist René Magritte. The seller was none other than Geffen, who had given the director a bargain price. When Spielberg learned this he asked Geffen why. "You are going to become a fanatic as an art collector," Geffen replied. "And I'm going to sit on the sidelines and enjoy watching you build your collection."

By 1990 Geffen was ready to sell his music label, but Warners—having just merged with Time Inc.—was in no position to pony up the money Geffen was expecting. Steve Ross sent emissaries urging Geffen to sign a new seven-year deal and look for his payday down the road. Geffen had no interest in that. He heard from several suitors before finally making a deal with Sidney Sheinberg, the MCA Universal executive who had given Spielberg his break. Geffen sold his company for $545 million in MCA stock.

Geffen turned fifty in 1993, and the party marking the occasion was held at the home of his now close friends Jeffrey and Marilyn Katzenberg. Geffen told the *Los Angeles Times* that he wasn't self-conscious about his age. "It's not a bummer, you know? It's nothing."

Now one of the richest self-made men in show business, Geffen could afford to dabble in various interests, including becoming an important link for the Democratic party and President Bill Clinton in Hollywood. Still, having started and sold two companies, he had to be wondering what was next.

Jeffrey Katzenberg, the youngest of the troika, was born December 21, 1950, in New York City. In classic Hollywood fashion he advanced by hitching himself to a bigger star, then proving himself able to take on more and more responsibilities. His first patron was Barry Diller, then chairman of Paramount Pictures. The fact that Katzenberg could thrive and advance under the acerbic Diller says much about his ambition—and his ability to endure in hopes of a long-term payoff. From doing things like smoothing Diller's way through customs, Katzenberg quickly developed a larger to-do list. When Diller announced that Paramount was launching a fourth television network in 1977, he was joined by both Michael Eisner, then Paramount's president and chief operating officer, and Katzenberg. The linchpin for the new network was to be a new *Star Trek* series, and Eisner and Katzenberg were two of the studio "suits" who worked with series creator Gene Roddenberry and his team. But the network—as then conceived—was never to be. The release of *Star Wars* that spring led Eisner to rethink the planned TV-movie pilot as a feature film. With the success of Spielberg's *Close Encounters* proving the new science-fiction boom wasn't a fluke, the network and revived TV series were dead, and what would become *Star Trek: The Motion Picture* was put into the pipeline.

Here's where Katzenberg proved his worth. Leonard Nimoy, the actor who had become famous as the half-human, half-Vulcan Mr. Spock, had no interest in joining the series after he received a halfhearted offer from Roddenberry to appear in only some episodes. A new character was created and cast to replace him; but once director Robert Wise was signed to do the feature film, things changed. When it was decided that the Spock character was essential for any *Trek* movie, it was Katzenberg whom Eisner sent to New York to meet with Nimoy, then appearing on Broadway in the hit play *Equus*. Over several days, whatever problems existed between Paramount, Roddenberry, and Nimoy were resolved, reportedly with a large check made out to Nimoy. This was not merely a war story from Katzenberg's early years. This was his *modus operandi*. He was so good at tracking down writers, directors, and actors and getting them to do what the studio needed them to do that he earned the nickname the "Golden Retriever."

In 1984 things had changed in Hollywood. The death of Charles Bluhdorn, the head of Gulf & Western, which then owned Paramount, meant that Diller no longer had someone in the corporate headquarters whom he trusted—or who trusted him. He moved to Twentieth Century Fox to run its studio, and was eventually instrumental in bringing in Rupert Murdoch to buy the company and finally launch the fourth broadcast network he had been denied at Paramount. Meanwhile Michael Eisner was also getting out. He was heading to the Walt Disney Company, which had just fought off a brutal takeover battle and now looked to Eisner to shake up a company that had grown lackluster and complacent while the rest of the industry was changing. Disney was still relying on traditional family films while audiences were thrilling to *Raiders of the Lost Ark* and *E.T.*

Eisner became chairman and CEO of Disney, and Katzenberg soon joined him as president of motion picture and television operations. Katzenberg thrived in his new job. Within days of taking over he announced that Disney would soon release its first R-rated film ever (through its new Touchstone division), *Down and Out in Beverly Hills*. He would demonstrate that Disney could be a major player in Hollywood, recruiting Martin Scorsese, Paul Newman, and Tom Cruise for *The Color of Money* and Bette Midler and Danny DeVito for *Ruthless People*, and selling a sitcom to NBC called *Golden Girls*. Katzenberg made the deal with ABC to launch a Sunday-night Disney movie. One of the very few stars he failed to retrieve for a project was Madonna.

It was Katzenberg who helped resuscitate Disney's animation unit. While the studio had continued turning out animated features in the years after founder Walt Disney's death in 1966, these films had been pale shadows of those in the studio's glory years. Under Katzenberg, Disney began producing animation that appealed to adults as well as kids: *The Little Mermaid*, *Who Framed Roger Rabbit*, *Beauty and the Beast*. He also made a deal with Pixar, a company that had made some computer-animated shorts, to begin work on feature films to be released through Disney. During his time there Katzenberg amassed an enviable track record. Eisner and Frank Wells (who ran the business side as president of the company) had been brought in by the shaken Disney board of directors in 1984 to turn the company around, and Katzenberg was entitled to a sizable bit of the credit for their success in doing so.

In April 1994 Hollywood was shocked to learn that Wells had died in a helicopter accident while on a ski vacation in Nevada. Even as funeral arrangements were being made, Wells's successor had to be selected. Katzenberg felt that, given his track record, the promotion was his due. He had worked his way up, bided his time, and accomplished a great deal. Many might say he had more than earned it, but Eisner disagreed. Whether it was jealousy over who deserved credit for what or simply a corporate power struggle is difficult to say, but the decision as to who would replace Wells became a Hollywood showdown. Katzenberg made it clear he wanted the job and would accept nothing less. He told David Geffen he would turn down an option that was worth some $100 million (and would keep him in his position for two more years) in order to show Eisner that he was serious about wanting the presidency of the whole operation. Geffen was aghast.

"Take the money and stay," advised Geffen. "Don't worry. It'll all work out."

On August 23, 1994, Katzenberg was summoned to Eisner's office for the moment of truth. Eisner handed him a press release announcing that Katzenberg had resigned from Disney. It was Eisner's way of telling him, "You're fired."

Katzenberg was forty-three. He was equipped to run a studio, but such jobs didn't open every day, and he had just been let go from the one place that did have such an opening. Friends like David Geffen and Steven Spielberg called to commiserate and suggest that perhaps better times were just ahead. Like them, Katzenberg was at a crossroads in his career.

2

Present at the Creation

WHEN JEFFREY KATZENBERG was shown the door at Disney, he was not without his fans. Although officially he was *persona non grata* at Disney, at several private parties the people he worked with had the chance, unofficially, to say goodbye. "Jeffrey was a believer in the corporate culture and a cheerleader," observed one producer, and those he cheered felt the loss.

Speculation was rife as to where Katzenberg might land. While there were not many opportunities for studio executives at the moment, Katzenberg was hardly the only one who was "at liberty." At summer's end in 1994, Barry Diller was still available after having helped in the founding of the FOX television network, while Mike Medavoy had recently resigned from Tri-Star Pictures. Jeff Sagansky, another Tri-Star alumnus, was at large, while Lucie Salhany, who had also had a tour of duty heading FOX TV, was now looking for a new job. *Variety*, noting the unusual amount of talent currently in the marketplace, had one more name to add to the mix: "And then there's the ultimate gadfly, David Geffen, who likes to trade rumors about who's going where, but has yet to make a major move himself."

From the start it was clear that the person who needed a new studio to run—who in many ways still needed to prove himself—was Jeffrey Katzenberg. Geffen and Steven Spielberg had enough money and power for several lifetimes, but Katzenberg was a man whose fate in the entertainment industry had repeatedly been determined by others. Thus it was no surprise that he yearned to run his own studio if he could find the right partners. His last day at Disney was September 22. He spent the day saying goodbye to those colleagues who did not feel disloyal in doing so, and, according to *Variety*, "table-hopping in the executive dining room."

What was clear to Katzenberg after his years at Paramount and Disney was that he was tired of linking his career to someone else's success. He felt it was time for him to be running a show himself. His friend Geffen was entirely supportive, telling him, "Start a company. Do what you want. You can do it."

Katzenberg had raised the notion with Spielberg, but Spielberg had a long and happy home at Universal. For years he had been under the benevolent wing of Sidney Sheinberg, who had brought him into the studio, and that was where his own production company, Amblin' Entertainment, had its offices. The turnover of industry ownership, however, had not left Universal unchanged. The company had been acquired by Matsushita (the Japanese firm best known for its electronics brand Panasonic), and Sheinberg was reportedly not happy under the new owners. If and when Sheinberg left, Spielberg's emotional tie to Universal would be severed, even if inertia kept him there. Suddenly Katzenberg's suggestion that they create their own reality in Hollywood didn't seem so far-fetched.

As their "what if" talk turned serious, Katzenberg suggested they needed someone who knew how to make financial deals and had grounding in those parts of the entertainment business that were beyond their scope. Katzenberg wasn't speculating. He was interested in bringing in his friend David Geffen, whose track record in wheeling and dealing, starting up and selling two music labels, as well as his not inconsiderable work in film and theater, made him a strong fit with the producer/director and the studio executive. Geffen, who was living nicely off his investments at this point, was happier being an outsider and working on charitable concerns, particularly those related to AIDS. But he allowed himself to be convinced by Katzenberg that there was nothing to lose by simply talking about a hypothetical start-up with him and Spielberg. When he showed up at Spielberg's home in Pacific Palisades, he was committed to nothing but conversation.

The notion of creating the first new studio in decades was intriguing and offered each of the three men something beyond what he had already achieved. For Katzenberg it was the opportunity to call his own shots. For Spielberg it was a chance to move beyond being a mere producer and director of films and enter the realm of the legendary moguls of the past: Louis B. Mayer, Samuel Goldwyn, David O. Selznick, Darryl F. Zanuck. For Geffen it was a whole new world to conquer, launching a multifaceted entertainment entity that would include not just music but film, television, video, and even interactive computer technology.

In late September fate found the three of them on the guest list at the White House where President Clinton was playing host to Russian president Boris Yeltsin. After the state dinner Spielberg and Katzenberg went to their rooms at the nearby Hay-Adams Hotel, but Geffen was a personal guest of the Clintons and had been invited to stay in the Lincoln Bedroom that evening. After a lengthy post-party conversation with Bill and Hillary Clinton, Geffen found that one couldn't simply leave the White House and go visiting elsewhere in Washington. It wasn't until the next morning that he was able to get away and meet with Spielberg and Katzenberg. When they finally got together, the idea came into focus, and the three decided to take the plunge. They would be forming their own new company.

Before it was announced, there were details to be hammered out. Spielberg went to Sidney Sheinberg for his blessing, and got it. In return Universal would end up as distributor for much of DreamWorks's output. Tellingly, Spielberg kept one foot out the door, reserving the right for himself to make movies for other studios, an option he would exercise repeatedly over the next several years.

Each of the three partners would have an equal investment in the company, which proved to be a problem for Katzenberg who had nowhere near the wealth of his two colleagues. Adding to the strain, his expected payout from Disney would not be forthcoming anytime soon because Michael Eisner was disputing the amount of $250 million that Katzenberg claimed he was owed for the projects he had initiated and overseen. (This argument over Katzenberg's claims eventually led to a protracted lawsuit.) In the end, each of the founders would put up $33.3 million, gaining a combined 67 percent share of the privately held company. The remaining third would be divided among outside investors who would have to put up considerably more. Simply on the strength of their names—and their track records—this new and as yet unnamed company would immediately be considered a player in the entertainment industry.

On October 12, 1994, Hollywood witnessed a historic press conference at the Peninsula Hotel in Beverly Hills. There reporters saw three middle-aged guys, none of whom had anything to prove, announce they were about to take a chance and do something that hadn't been done in nearly sixty years. They were launching a new movie studio. They didn't have a location. They hadn't come up with a name. Indeed, the industry press scratched its collective head and tried to figure out what the real story was. Could this be Katzenberg getting his revenge on Eisner? Was this an elaborate ruse by Sheinberg and MCA Universal chairman Lew Wasserman to wrest Universal away from Matsushita? Was this really a stalking horse for Microsoft to invade Hollywood? (There had been reports of Katzenberg meeting with Bill Gates.)

The phrase immediately slapped on the project, with Katzenberg's approval, was the "Dream Team." It was Katzenberg who looked at his partners at the press conference and said, "I look at the three of us, and I figure this has gotta be the Dream Team. Certainly it's my Dream Team."

Arnold Rifkin, head of the motion picture division of the William Morris Agency, said, "Look who they are and look what they've done. Because of their names they enter the studio business on an even playing field." Alan Horn, one of the founders of Castle Rock Films, was only a bit more reserved: "From the standpoint of getting talent, they are starting with three big rockets in Jeffrey, Steven and David. But the majors still have a clear advantage, and that's a library of titles to provide cash flow and sustain overhead."

Variety editor-in-chief Peter Bart, himself a former studio executive, was bemused by the announcement and shared his concerns in his column. "[Y]ou were unprepared to talk about your business plan, your financial structure—you didn't even have a name for your new enterprise," he wrote. "I realize you've talked about 'building an asset' and creating 'true autonomy,' but . . . don't all of you already have all the assets and all the autonomy you could ever want?"

Also baffling was who would be in charge. The three told the assembled reporters that everything would be shared; Geffen even joked he would be directing the sequel to Spielberg's *Jurassic Park*. The fact was that having reached step one, they hadn't thought much about step two. Now they had to determine how they would begin doing all the things they wanted to do, including making films, recordings, TV shows, and computer games.

It was going to take a lot of money.

Katzenberg had hoped to keep everything a secret until the announcement. He intended to come out and say that he wanted to introduce his partners before revealing why he had called everyone in. Then Spielberg and Geffen would step out to everyone's shock and amazement. Unfortunately Hollywood is no better at keeping secrets than Washington, and the news leaked out the preceding day. That didn't put a crimp in media interest, but it did have an interesting side effect. Among the many calls the three received after the news first broke were offers upon offers to invest in the new company.

Talking about money was one thing, putting it up was another. The still unnamed company began making its first deals in early 1995. First was an unprecedented agreement for a television production partnership with Capital Cities/ABC. Unprecedented was that the new studio intended to produce shows not only for the ABC network but for other outlets as well. In addition the Dream Team would get a share of the advertising revenue. It was the sort of creative deal-making that the troika had said would be their hallmark, with the promise of five prime-time shows and four first-run syndicated programs to be produced by the joint venture over the next seven years.

That same January they also settled on a name for the company. It would be known as DreamWorks SKG, with the initials standing for the names of each of the partners. *Variety*'s Peter Bart noted that they "certainly have no need to prove their credentials to the Hollywood establishment; they *are* the establishment."

The newly christened DreamWorks, with the Cap Cities/ABC deal in its pocket, soon had more announcements. Paul Allen—a co-founder of Microsoft with Bill Gates—said he was investing $500 million in the company, declaring, "I always wanted to be in the entertainment business." (Allen was already an investor in Ticketmaster and the Portland Trailblazers basketball team, among other ventures.)

A few days later it was Gates's turn to partner with DreamWorks, announcing a co-venture on DreamWorks Interactive, which would include CD ROMs, video games and other interactive adventures for the family market. Each would contribute $15 million, apart from an additional $9 million Microsoft was reported to be invested in DreamWorks itself. "The potential for combining the incredible stories created by Jeffrey, Steven and David with the innovative technology and amazing interactivity that are possible today and in the future is just awesome to me," Gates enthused.

Now DreamWorks was ready to get down to specifics. It planned to have three feature films ready for release by the next year, five in 1997, and by 2000 nine a year. Dream-Works Interactive would release three to five titles by the end of 1996 and a dozen more the following year. And the money and deals and announcements kept rolling in. DreamWorks would have its films released internationally by UIP, a joint venture of Universal and Paramount, except in South Korea. (The reason for that odd blip is that One World Media Corp. put up $300 million for a 10.8 percent stake in the company and in return received exclusive South Korean rights to DreamWorks's releases.) Chemical Bank put together a consortium that underwrote a ten-year billion-dollar revolving line of credit for the studio. It seemed everyone was lining up to toss money at Dream-Works. Said one potential lender, "For banks interested in lending to the media, this deal is almost a must." It was a very good position to be in for a start-up enterprise, and it was based solely on the star power of the troika, plus the support they already had from Cap Cities, Allen, and Gates.

In March the DreamWorks team, which had yet to produce a reel of film, made the cover of *Time* magazine. The weekly tried to report on the hype and got caught up in a bit of it themselves, citing the company's potential as "the prototype plugged-in multimedia company of the new millennium."

The story also touched on the slightly unequal footing among the investors. Paul Allen had a worth of some $4 *billion*. His hefty $500 million investment was something he could spare. Geffen and Spielberg were not in that league, but Geffen's worth was estimated to be in the neighborhood of some $600 million, so his $33 million stake would not require him to brown-bag his lunches. Katzenberg, on the other hand, while not quite living paycheck to paycheck, *felt* his investment by having to take out a mortgage to come up with his share. "I have not just figuratively bet the ranch," he told *Time*. "I have literally bet the ranch. My entire net worth is riding on the success of this company."

Not surprisingly, the earliest titles announced as future DreamWorks projects were in the animation division, which was under Katzenberg's purview: *Prince of Egypt* and *El Dorado*. On the live-action side it was announced that Walter Parkes and Laurie MacDonald, the husband-and-wife team who had been working with Spielberg at Amblin', would move to DreamWorks to run the film division. They wouldn't have any titles, though. No one would. Nor would there be any organizational flow chart. And when those dreamy profits came in down the road, they would be shared with everyone. To some it sounded like anarchy, but Geffen had managed to bring in Paul Allen and Chemical Bank, and Katzenberg had clinched the deal with ABC, and Spielberg was . . . well, he was Steven Spielberg. If anyone could do what they planned, these were the guys who should be able to do it.

Yet oddly it was Spielberg, the one with the most star power and the least business acumen, who was the most nervous about their prospects. In a revealing comment he admitted they might be trying to do too much too soon. "We could have built this up over a fifteen-year period. Instead, we're trying to do it in a couple of years. After our first planning sessions, I thought about how much easier it would be to start with a single film, make it, see how it does, and if it does well, do a second picture. That's the conservative, play-it-safe side that haunts me before I fall asleep at night."

Something in the enterprise truly excited Spielberg, though, and perhaps his partners let him push his plans forward as a way of keeping him happy. DreamWorks would give them the opportunity to build a brand-new state-of-the-art studio facility for the twenty-first century. That would make the dream real.

3

A Room of One's Own

IN RETROSPECT, the proposed DreamWorks Studio at Playa Vista seems like a metaphor for the company. It was a grand scheme that, had it succeeded, might well have transformed the industry. Going in with high hopes and support from some major players, there was every reason to expect the Dream Team to accomplish what it said it planned to do. Instead not one building would ever be erected for this studio of the future. The miscalculations and hubris that went into the project may have revealed more about DreamWorks than anything it actually accomplished.

The world learned of DreamWorks's grand plan on December 13, 1995. On that day the troika held another press conference—a scant fourteen months after their initial debut and without a single movie or TV show yet in release—unveiling a project as grand as DreamWorks itself. It was the DreamWorks Studio at Playa Vista, with groundbreaking set for June 1996. As described, this thousand-acre facility would be unlike any studio Hollywood had ever seen. Not only would DreamWorks have its movie production facilities and offices there, but computer companies like IBM,

Silicon Graphics, and Digital Domain would have operations there as well, the better to be involved in joint projects with DreamWorks. The studio was scheduled to open by the end of 1998 or early 1999, and the facility would also include retail shops, office space for other businesses, and more than 3,200 residences. It was a project expected to create 8,000 jobs.

At the press conference the excitement at this major announcement was palpable. It came from the presence not only of the troika but of California governor Pete Wilson and Los Angeles mayor Richard Riordan. Rumors circulated that DreamWorks investor Bill Gates might appear, and such was the hype that some thought this would be a worthy venue for President Bill Clinton. Neither Gates nor Clinton showed.

Nonetheless Governor Wilson was ecstatic, even by the standards of politicians taking credit for something they have nothing to do with. "I'm pleased as hell," he said. "In my previous incarnation as mayor I would have sold my children to get a project like this."

The city of Los Angeles was equally ecstatic. To encourage DreamWorks in this joint venture (there were to be other partners as well), the city dished out $70 million in incentives—a combination of tax breaks, discounts on permits, and a waiver of $40 million in road construction and improvements. The facility was scheduled to include a 42,000-square-foot soundstage, reckoned to be the world's largest, as well as 20 additional soundstages for film and television production. There would be 2 million square feet in production and post-production space for various tenants. Already prepared to sign up were such people as James Cameron, director of *Titanic*, and Stan Winston, one of the biggest names in the world of special effects. GTE would install a fiber-optic high-capacity network that would be available to everyone on what was being billed as the "campus." Indeed, attendees were told, this would be the "prototype community of the future."

While Geffen and Katzenberg may have had private reservations about the cost—they noted that building a studio was Spielberg's initiative—they were on board now. Geffen noted, "Most of the other studios were built when people were still driving Model T's. The technology has passed them by." Spielberg was like a kid in a roomful of presents, on the verge of having his dreams come true: "There's an electricity on a movie lot that goes through your clothes. Your heart beats faster. That's what we wanted."

With the announcement of all these grand schemes, someone might have thought of a better place to have the press conference. While they wanted to do it on site, holding it in the hangar where Howard Hughes had housed his infamous Spruce Goose—a wooden cargo transport plane that never did the job it was built to do—proved to be a much more important omen of things to come than anything said that day.

Playa Vista was the largest remaining unbuilt tract in the city of Los Angeles. It is located on the city's west side and for years had been owned by Howard Hughes. During World War II it had been used to build aircraft. After Hughes's death the property was sold, but the building that had once housed the Spruce Goose remained. The property owners did a bit of farming on the land, not out of any desire to get back to nature but because farm land was taxed at a lower rate. A few years before DreamWorks appeared on the scene, the land was acquired by a joint venture of

Los Angeles developers known as Maguire-Thomas Partners. They were interested in building and developing the
property, but a number of issues had to be resolved since
the property extended toward the Pacific Coast and included some wetlands.

Ruth Galanter, elected to the Los Angeles City Council in
1987, represented the district containing the site. Trained as
an urban planner, her goal was to protect the wetlands and
yet allow the development to continue. She would be a big
booster of the Playa Vista project, much to the consterna-
tion of some environmentalists who wanted no development at all there. It was Galanter who convinced the developers to include residential use in the mix instead of
making it strictly commercial. She also saw some possibilities when Maguire-Thomas began renting the old Hughes
hangar for movie production.

"After the '94 earthquake in LA, which destroyed a number of soundstages, mainly in the San Fernando Valley,
Maguire-Thomas found a use for the Spruce Goose hangar.
They were using it as a soundstage and renting it out. It
was, I think at the time, the only income on the property,"
she recalled. "And none of the neighbors ever complained,
which is what was significant to me as a City Council member. I never heard a peep out of any of the people who live
on the bluff above it, or people who lived in the surrounding area. . . . I think nobody even knew."

Most appealing about the use of the site for a soundstage was that people in the movie business don't commute
during rush hours, so they wouldn't add to the traffic when
nonindustry residents were trying to get to work. One day
Galanter heard from someone at Maguire-Thomas, asking
if she'd like to meet Steven Spielberg. Although she was in
municipal government, not the movie industry, she readily

agreed, but she wondered what the occasion was. Maguire-Thomas said they wanted to show off the land as a potential site for DreamWorks. Having the city government on board at this early stage would obviously make it more appealing.

So the developers built a platform out in the middle of the property and took the DreamWorks crew out to see for themselves. Galanter recalled, "We could point to places, 'Steven, there's where your studio is going to be.'" They were sold, or at least Spielberg was, and Katzenberg began negotiations with the city and the developers to get the best deal they could. Galanter made it clear that the city wanted to give them all the breaks they could, but this would not be a free ride. "Look, if we're going to do public subsidies for the three richest white guys in the universe, we've got to get something for it," she told them. What she got was a commitment from DreamWorks for a program to open up jobs for minorities and others who didn't have an entree to the entertainment world. (As it turned out, the industry was coming under increasing fire for erecting barriers against minorities who wanted to break into the business, so DreamWorks was going with the tide by agreeing to do something to change it. The company set up a program which it initially funded, then got additional support from private and public sources.)

With everyone on board for the Playa Vista project, the carping of some private environmental groups was thought to be a minor speed bump. The *Los Angeles Business Journal*, in an expansive article about plans for the property, informed its readers, "[T]he City Council gave its final approval to the [zoning] changes Nov. 3, but that decision was appealed by a group calling itself Save Ballona Wetlands. The City Council will take up that appeal on Dec. 8—the final hurdle in the plan's approval."

Thus would begin an ordeal that would tie up everyone involved in the project, tarnish the reputations of the DreamWorks principals as heartless businessmen out to despoil the environment for personal gain, and finally force them to walk away from the deal. Years later successor developers continue the fight to do something with the land, but the saga of the failed DreamWorks studio was a costly lesson in how not everyone in the world was about to roll over for Spielberg, Katzenberg, and Geffen.

Bruce Robertson, a private investigator and one of the environmental activists, recalled the dismissive treatment they received in the face of the DreamWorks publicity machine. "Initially they tried to paint us as rabble rousers and tried to discredit us. Spielberg didn't make any public comments. Both Geffen and Katzenberg made disparaging comments about us when we had various news conferences and protests at their events," he said.

Actually Robertson, who was one of a coalition of activists opposing the development, may have forgotten a Spielberg gibe made early on. Commenting on the numerous wildlife that made the Ballona Wetlands their home, Spielberg told a news conference, "I also welcome any frog in Los Angeles to please come to Playa Vista. When the wetlands are complete, you have a home here, too." Spielberg's grin—and the loud laughter that greeted this invitation—made it clear just how little the DreamWorks people thought of the environmental claims.

Robertson and other activists knew that DreamWorks's involvement had turned an essentially local dispute about a real estate development into a story with real star power.

The environmentalists took advantage of that, much to the chagrin of people like City Councilor Galanter, who had won office pledging to bring environmental concerns to bear on local development. "It was particularly galling to have a bunch of people come in and claim, falsely, that the studio was going to be built in the wetlands," she said. "Suddenly there's this news opportunity and they are everywhere, accusing Steven Spielberg of slaughtering frogs. . . . We do have endangered species in the wetlands, but the studio wasn't in the wetlands, it was a mile and a half away. In between, essentially, is urban Los Angeles."

It would take several years for DreamWorks to realize it was in the middle of a public relations battle, and one it was losing badly. By the summer of 1996 it was no closer to breaking ground than it had been six months earlier, but on paper the future studio continued to attract attention in the industry. It was exciting because new production facilities on this scale hadn't been built in Hollywood in more than half a century. This time, with Spielberg's involvement, it would be a studio constructed with input from someone who had actually made movies. The soundstages would have removable skylights to allow natural sunlight onto sets, and each building would be separate, to allow loading and unloading from all four sides. Among other innovations planned were fully automated lighting grids as well as water tanks available on each soundstage for scenes taking place in, on, or under water. Spielberg said the tanks were "something all directors are crying for." That may sound odd to the lay person, who assumes such scenes take place in whatever watery location the script describes, but the director of *Jaws* knew what the controlled environment of a water tank could provide to filmmakers. The hope was that work would finally begin on the dream studio by the end of the year.

A few months later the groundbreaking was still in the indefinite future, and the DreamWorks folks weren't talking to the press about it any more. The key delay, said the developers, was putting together the financing for this massive undertaking. There were significant problems. The developers had outstanding debts from the decades they had spent trying to develop the property. Further, an analysis of what lessees would have to be charged for space in order for the project to make economic sense was coming out at about thirty dollars per square foot—substantially higher than what was being charged in the Los Angeles market at the time. Still, everyone was upbeat.

Steve McDonald, director of the city's economic development group, told the local media, "There are lots of smart people at DreamWorks and at Maguire-Thomas, and we remain confident that they can put this thing together."

Yet summer turned to fall and fall closed in on winter, and the news remained rocky. DreamWorks's first movies were still at least a year away. Initial TV offerings were foundering. And the company was no closer to starting construction on the studio than it had been on the day of the announcement. The story now began attracting national attention outside of the trade press. Bruce Robertson was not only talking to local media, he was being quoted in *U.S. News and World Report* in a story about the struggles over Playa Vista. Commenting on all the incentives DreamWorks had received from the city, Robertson said, "Talk about corporate welfare—tens of millions in tax breaks to DreamWorks. I don't think anyone thought they were going to go to Boise. This wasn't necessary to 'keep' them in Los Angeles." Worse was the pessimistic prediction by an anonymous DreamWorks employee: "I probably won't be working for the company by the time it gets its own studio."

The project was further delayed when things began falling apart for the managing partner of the developers, Robert F. Maguire III. Both Katzenberg and Galanter blamed Maguire for the delays, and it turned out that this wasn't his only project beset by problems. Katzenberg threatened to pull out of the deal completely. "We're not waiting any longer for these people to sort out their mess," he said, adding that DreamWorks would begin considering other locations for its studio. "We've waited for a year already, and we need to find a home for our company."

Meanwhile the environmental issues were not going away. Katzenberg dismissed them, but the activists kept going to court, appealing when they lost, and keeping the litigation alive. "Most conventional lenders will not finance a construction project with a lawsuit outstanding," said Peter Denniston, Playa Vista's project manager. No one could connect the dots directly between the complaints and the problems the developer was facing, but the various groups took credit for putting sand in the gears and slowing things to the point where nothing was moving.

Then, at the beginning of 1997, it looked like Playa Vista might be rejuvenated. Maguire was out and Gary Winnick, chairman of the Pacific Capital Group, an investment firm headquartered in Beverly Hills, was in. It was DreamWorks that led to Winnick's taking over the project. Pacific Capital was doing some unrelated work for the studio, and Winnick got to meet several of the executives. Apparently they liked what they saw. Coming at the time the relationship with Maguire was souring, it seemed like the sort of fortuitous meeting that happens only in the movies. It didn't hurt that Winnick had big investment money behind him, including union pension funds, that allowed him to outmaneuver other suitors for the development. The deal would be formally closed in May, and then, after a few minor details were cleaned up—like those environmental suits—work could finally begin on the studio.

That same January the battle over the Ballona Wetlands made *Premiere* magazine. The story was about how Hollywood greens had yet to embrace the cause, whether it was because they were afraid of offending potential employers at DreamWorks or, just as likely, because they hadn't heard about it. But over several pages, *Premiere*'s readers got to see photos of protesters with signs reading, "Don't Let Ballona Become Another Jurassic Park" and "Save Wetland Critters—E.T. Would Approve." Even in a town where there was supposed to be no such thing as bad publicity, this was bad news. As the writer Jeff Stockwell astutely noted, the big corporation facing the powerless citizens trying to save nature was a story Hollywood told often, but the "guy behind the bulldozer . . . isn't supposed to win."

By that fall there was still no groundbreaking. DreamWorks had managed to lease New York City office space for its marketing and distribution staff, and its first feature film, *The Peacemaker*, was finally released in September, only a year behind schedule. *Variety* ran a major examination of where DreamWorks stood as it approached its third birthday, but now the troika was nowhere to be found, making themselves unavailable for interviews. The trade paper, long known as the "Bible of Show Business," took the unusual step of criticizing the studio for "haughtiness" for refusing to cooperate with the article. Still, it was beginning to look like the Playa Vista studio would finally happen, with construction set to begin in June 1998.

More months went by, and suddenly the developers and DreamWorks found themselves on opposing sides. The city had tied all its financial concessions to the establishment of

DreamWorks in Playa Vista, and in a new negotiating stance DreamWorks now argued that in return for being the anchor for the whole project, the developers ought to give the studio fifty acres for its facilities at no cost. The developers were outraged, having already agreed to sell them the land at below market value. To give it away, they felt, would be a betrayal of their investors, and now that there were pension funds involved, those investors could be fairly characterized as the proverbial widows and orphans. City Councilor Galanter sided with the studio, with Adi Lieberman, her chief of staff, telling the press, "Any time a developer is asking for government incentives, Galanter has to ask herself what the community receives in return. The new owners haven't come up with an affordable housing mix, and haven't struck a deal with DreamWorks, so she couldn't in good conscience give away the people's resources for free."

Unsaid was what Galanter knew from behind-the-scenes conversations with Katzenberg. DreamWorks was getting cold feet about the whole project, and he didn't think it could come up with sufficient financing to build the studio facility. "Jeffrey told me several times in the months leading up to the pullout that his financial people were telling the three guys not to do this. The basic argument described to me by Katzenberg was, 'Look fellas, you haven't even made a movie yet. You really can't, the company can't, afford to do this. You three guys want to do it with your own money, that's fine, but we can't afford to do this.'"

Why did DreamWorks stay at it? One reason is that Spielberg really wanted it, and it was important to keep him happy. On paper the only thing he was really committed to at DreamWorks was his initial investment. He was supposed to make movies for the studio, but he wasn't obligated to, and nothing prevented him from making movies for competing studios. When Spielberg examined the property more closely he was thrilled. On one visit he got up on a crane to see the "view" from where his future office would be built. So there were competing pressures even within DreamWorks itself.

In August 1998 Katzenberg sent a detailed letter to the developers accusing them of trying to change the deal and making it clear that though DreamWorks was the anchor for this development, nothing prevented the studio from walking away. "DreamWorks will have no choice but to begin working with the city to secure a new home elsewhere," wrote Katzenberg. In an indication of how badly things had deteriorated, Peter Denniston, now president of Playa Capital, which was running the project, answered, "If DreamWorks cannot agree to come to Playa Vista, we will move aggressively to bring another studio or studios to the project."

A month later things had calmed a bit. DreamWorks agreed to pay $20 million for the land, and it would allow Playa Capital to rent out some soundstages to outsiders. It was Ruth Galanter who got them talking, telling them, "You're supposed to be dealmakers! Make a deal!" The deal was completed in November—nearly three years after the original announcement—with DreamWorks to pay $20 million and receive outright ownership of forty-seven acres.

But the bad publicity didn't stop. Beyond the environs of Los Angeles the fight over Playa Vista had been reported by CNN, NBC Nightly News, *The Nation*, *Mother Jones*, and other outlets who saw the battle as one between feisty but powerless activists and powerful real estate and political interests allied with DreamWorks. California state senator Tom Hayden, an opponent of the development, made it clear why he thought some environmentalists were sitting out the fight: "They think of Spielberg as a good guy and [DreamWorks] SKG as a million-dollar contributor to liberal causes. It simply makes environmentalists uncomfortable to get into a fight with these fellows."

Finally, in the summer of 1999—nearly four years after the initial announcement—DreamWorks pulled out of the deal. There would be no studio of the future after all. The developers would continue to try to build on the land, but it would be without Spielberg and company, and without the tax incentives that had been linked to DreamWorks building a studio there. Said Spielberg, "Building our own studio has been a dream for Jeffrey, David and me since the inception of our company, and not building at Playa Vista in no way deters us from that goal." Yet an unnamed source "close to the talks" told *Variety* that this had been a great deal for DreamWorks and something unrelated to the development had caused them to pull back. "Playa Capital practically gave them the land. All they had to do was come up with their own construction financing," said the anonymous source. "I think DreamWorks either didn't have the dough, or they decided maybe they didn't want to do it after all."

The local media fingered David Geffen as the person who didn't want to spend the money and Spielberg as the one fixated on a studio that, in the end, didn't make much sense for a start-up operation. In an official statement Katzenberg, reportedly the man in the middle who was ready to proceed if it made sense but wasn't married to the notion the way Spielberg was, tried to put the best face on it: "We have learned a great deal during the past four years and it is clear that this move was no longer in DreamWorks's best interest. It was simply not meant to be."

DreamWorks remained in its offices at Universal, but in an odd footnote to the collapsed deal, it did get a new facility for its animation division. Katzenberg had told Ruth Galanter that the studio needed to set up its animation shop in the San Fernando Valley. "None of the animators would cross the hill. So they were looking for a site in the Valley for the animation unit," she recalled. "The city of Los Angeles Department of Water and Power owned a piece of property in the city of Glendale in the San Fernando Valley that was not in use . . . [and] we sold them the piece of property where their animation studio is, outside the city of Los Angeles." It was doubly disappointing because all the dealing was meant to get DreamWorks to invest and hire within Los Angeles.

As for the environmental activists, Robertson believes their protests—which took place not only at the Playa Vista site but at DreamWorks premieres and other Hollywood events—had begun to take their toll. Whatever the future of the Playa Vista site post-DreamWorks, the saga was clearly an embarrassment to the studio. Although it was about to embark on its headiest years in filmmaking, the studio that wasn't may have been a predictor of DreamWorks's future. The Dream Team dreamed big but couldn't deliver. Looking back, Robertson wondered if the collapse of the deal wasn't "a kind of microcosm of the DreamWorks story."

4

Movies to Go

ACTOR TOM HANKS, being friendly with each member of the troika, was asked in *Time* magazine's 1995 cover story on DreamWorks to guess whether it would succeed or fail. Known as a genuine nice guy, but not without an impish sense of humor, he replied, "I guarantee that, when their first film premieres, everyone will say, 'This is it? This is what these three geniuses have come up with?' Unless it immediately enters the pantheon as one of the three highest-grossing films of all time, everybody will ask what's the big deal."

Everyone understood it would take some time for DreamWorks to get up to speed. But as 1995 turned into 1996 and still no movies appeared, skeptics wondered what was taking so long. From the beginning Katzenberg seemed eager to maintain the hype while at the same time lowering expectations. "There is no road map, no guidebook for us to look and say, 'This is where we're going.' It's still evolving." The hope was to have the company's first films out by December 1996—not an unreasonable expectation.

Of course it wasn't simply a matter of making movies and booking them into theaters. DreamWorks didn't aim to be merely an independent production company but a full-blown studio. That meant it would also have to manage the distribution of its films, which included not only booking them into theaters but overseeing the marketing of each release. This was not the glamorous side of the business. Critics and movie fans may not pay much attention to these nuts and bolts of the movie industry, but they were crucial if DreamWorks was to be a full-service studio.

Producers Dino DeLaurentiis and Jerry Weintraub had made attempts in the 1980s to set up their own production and distribution operations (with, respectively, the DeLaurentiis Entertainment Group and the Weintraub Entertainment Group). Both failed. The people at DreamWorks decided early on to farm out international distribution, cutting a deal with UIP, which handled foreign sales for several companies. In North America, however, DreamWorks intended to release its own films. This amounted to a $10 million to $15 million operation starting from scratch, and it made sense only if the studio had enough films in the pipeline to make it worth the money and effort and, most important, start the revenue stream flowing back to the studio.

By late 1995 DreamWorks was buying up movie rights to various properties (its first purchase was the Michael Crichton novel *Neanderthal*) as well as putting its animation unit to work on what was anticipated to be a prestige holiday release three or four years down the road, *Prince of Egypt*. The first seven minutes of *Prince* were screened for the DreamWorks staff before year's end to let them know there were movies in production and there would be plenty to do soon enough.

Finally in March 1996 the studio's first live-action feature got the green light. It was, of all things, a run-of-the-mill action-oriented thriller called *The Peacemaker*. The movie would mark the film debut of Mimi Leder, a director who had television credits going back a decade, including several episodes of *E.R.* Annette Bening was reportedly in talks for the female lead, a civilian nuclear physicist who joins forces with an American colonel (to be played by George Clooney) to track down a missing Russian nuclear missile. The part would eventually go to Nicole Kidman. Sight unseen, it certainly didn't sound like a candidate for Hanks's pantheon of great films.

Major studios release all kinds of movies, from serious Oscar contenders to cheesy horror films to family comedies. But the first film from DreamWorks presented an opportunity for a major studio to announce that it would not be doing business as usual. Instead, the troika chose a project that could have come from any of the other players in Hollywood.

Film projects continued to be announced. There would be an animated feature called *El Dorado*. A green light was given to a family film about a girl and a parrot, entitled *Paulie*. Rights were picked up for $500,000 to a children's picture book by William Steig about an ogre named Shrek. Perhaps something might pop out and be a surprise hit, but where was DreamWorks's star filmmaker Steven Spielberg? Why wasn't he directing one of the studio's premiere efforts?

As it turns out, Spielberg was preoccupied, working on his first film since the Oscar-winning *Schindler's List*. It was *The Lost World: Jurassic Park*, which would be one of the smash hits of the summer of 1997. Unfortunately for DreamWorks, it would be a hit for Universal Pictures and Spielberg's Amblin' Entertainment. Of course he couldn't have made the film for DreamWorks because they didn't own the rights, but it was a clear assertion of Spielberg's priorities that his first movie since the DreamWorks announcement in 1994 would be for a rival studio, even if Universal was also DreamWorks's landlord.

Perhaps Walter Parkes and Laurie MacDonald, who were riding herd on the DreamWorks film division, had some other project they could get into the pipeline? It turned out they did. It was *Men in Black*, another summer blockbuster, only this was something they had had in development at Columbia. It was understood that all three had prior commitments to clear up, but as *Entertainment Weekly* noted in its appraisal of DreamWorks after three years, "Although Hollywood was expecting it to act like a studio, DreamWorks was still operating like a production company. Parkes and MacDonald were in charge of day-to-day filmmaking activities, but they also functioned as producers on *Peacemaker* and Spielberg's upcoming *Amistad*—responsibilities rarely assumed by other studio heads like Disney's Joe Roth or Universal's Ron Meyer. As a result, the two execs were spread dangerously thin."

The question also persisted as to why Jeffrey Katzenberg seemed to be shut out of the live-action side of the studio. His answer was that the troika consulted but had divided responsibilities, and they all lived with that. Said Katzenberg, "In three years we haven't had an argument, much less a fight."

Katzenberg remained the odd man out. He most needed DreamWorks to work—to make his fortune, to show he could run a studio—and thus was at a disadvantage in dealing with Spielberg and Geffen. Spielberg wanted his studio, so they were pursuing Playa Vista. They both wanted Katzenberg to tone down his previously tenacious and combative style, and he did so. Said Geffen, "Jeffrey's become much more user-friendly."

As it turned out, Spielberg's next few films would be for DreamWorks, or at least a partnership between Dream-Works and another studio. Spielberg and Tom Hanks planned to work together on *Saving Private Ryan*, an expensive World War II film that would be a co-production between DreamWorks and Paramount, which owned the script. As movies had become increasingly expensive, such partnerships were becoming more frequent, with all sorts of deals worked out on how expenses—and income—were to be divided. Usually the big sticking point was dividing up distribution, with one company getting domestic rights and the other handling the film around the world. Domestic distribution was the plum because it carried bragging rights for the film. When *A Beautiful Mind* won the Oscar for best picture of 2001, it was as a Universal film, since the Ron Howard–directed project was handled in the United States by that studio. In fact the film was a co-production with DreamWorks, but no one in Hollywood counted it as a win for DreamWorks too. Even as DreamWorks shared in the money, industry perceptions remained important.

There are many ways the parties can negotiate the deal, but on *Saving Private Ryan* Spielberg was up against a man more powerful than even he was: Sumner Redstone, who as chairman of Viacom called the shots at Paramount, CBS, and numerous other entities in the Viacom empire. With neither side wanting to cede domestic distribution, they decided to determine it by a flip of a coin. Spielberg called tails, supposedly having had a premonition that would be the right call.

Uh uh, said Redstone. You flip the coin, *I'll* make the call.

Spielberg flipped the quarter. Redstone called heads. It came up tails. And that's how DreamWorks got what would eventually become its first prestige hit.

Although it had already premiered some TV shows (see the next chapter), DreamWorks was considered first and foremost a movie studio. As the third anniversary of its founding approached, it was finally preparing to release its first film, Leder's *The Peacemaker*. Also set for release before year end were two other films as different from each other as both were from *The Peacemaker*. Nathan Lane, Lee Evans, and Christopher Walken starred in *Mousehunt*, a raucous comedy about two brothers (Lane and Evans) who inherit a potentially valuable mansion infested with a very persistent mouse. It was directed by Gore Verbinski, who would score a later hit, *The Ring*, for DreamWorks and the highly successful *Pirates of the Caribbean* for Disney. And finally showing that he was indeed committed to DreamWorks, Steven Spielberg had directed a historical drama about slavery entitled *Amistad*.

On paper it looked great, as if DreamWorks had spread its bets across the board—a commercial thriller, a wacky comedy, and a prestige historical production from the director of *Schindler's List*. As each film was different, each would ultimately fail in its own way. Fortunately none of them was a big bet. Where *Prince of Egypt*, now set for a December 1998 release, was expected to cost an estimated $70 million, none of the live-action entries came close. *The Peacemaker* was the most expensive at $50 million, *Amistad* the cheapest at $36 million. DreamWorks took out ads trumpeting its first three releases, declaring that its new studio had finally arrived.

The Peacemaker arrived to lukewarm reviews. Some critics noted as a matter of course that it was the first offering from DreamWorks. Some assessed the status of Clooney's or Kidman's still budding Hollywood movie careers. Some picked up on the fact that DreamWorks had put a first-time woman director in charge of what was traditionally thought to be a male preserve: the muscular action film. Charles Taylor, film critic for the on-line magazine *Salon*, commented, "If you pick up this month's *Elle*, you can see a short profile of Leder under the headline 'Action Woman: Director Mimi Leder Plays with the Big Boys,' the implication being: Isn't it great that a first-time woman director gets to work in a genre usually reserved for men? I suppose so, if you think that it's a leap forward for woman filmmakers to get a chance to prove they can be as brutal and stupid as men."

In a way, Taylor had noted something that would become a hallmark at DreamWorks over the years. In an industry in which women long had to struggle to break into the boys' clubs, DreamWorks would be different. Women were given major positions of authority. Laurie MacDonald was co-head of film production. Terry Press ruled the studio's publicity machine. Even Leder would come out okay, going from *The Peacemaker* into *Deep Impact*, a Paramount/DreamWorks co-production for the summer of 1998.

Still, reading the tea leaves to try to predict the future of the film's participants didn't make people want to go see it. Roger Ebert was kind, noting that it looked great even if the material consisted mostly of retreads from other movies. *Variety*'s Todd McCarthy dismissed it as "an uncommonly dour and even grim action thriller." It took in less than $42 million on domestic release, which didn't even cover the cost of production, much less prints and advertising. (The rough Hollywood rule of thumb is that a movie must make at least three times its production cost to break even. Of course, anyone who has ever been in business with Hollywood reports that there's often more creativity in the accounting than in what appears on screen.) It made another $60 million overseas, and when home-video, cable, television, and other sales were added, it wasn't a disaster. But as Tom Hanks might have noted, it wasn't a candidate for a list of the greatest films ever made either. Nonetheless, in spite of the disappointment, DreamWorks took out the expected ads in the trade press trumpeting that its first release had a "worldwide gross" of $100 million.

Next up was *Mousehunt*, a loud, vulgar, and overlong (even if only ninety-seven minutes) slapstick comedy that had even its partisans eventually saying enough was enough. It did better than *Peacemaker* at the box office, by about $20 million, largely on the strength of appealing to kids during the December school vacation period. It was quickly forgotten.

Now the pressure was on *Amistad*, a serious story about how former president John Quincy Adams (played by Oscar-winning actor Anthony Hopkins) went to court to free African natives who had survived a brutal and harrowing journey on a slave ship. Here was the film that would surely announce the arrival of the studio, perhaps earning Steven Spielberg another Oscar nomination, but certainly cementing his reputation as a serious filmmaker capable of more than special-effects movies with space aliens or computer-generated dinosaurs.

Unfortunately for DreamWorks, a woman named Barbara Chase-Riboud was very upset about the film. She knew the story well, having written a 1989 novel on the subject of the *Amistad* slave ship. In November 1997, just weeks before the opening of the film, she went to court to get an injunction against DreamWorks to prevent them from releasing a film she claimed infringed on her copyright.

Barbara Chase-Riboud, then fifty-eight, hadn't planned on derailing DreamWorks. Indeed, her interests were far removed from Hollywood. She was an artist and writer who had sold a set of prints to the Museum of Modern Art while still in high school. Her sculptures are part of the permanent collections of the Metropolitan Museum of Art in New York and the Centre Pompidou in Paris. She was also an award-winning novelist and poet, specializing in historical themes. Her first novel, *Sally Hemmings*, was about the black slave reputed to be the mistress of Thomas Jefferson.

It was her third novel that led to the lawsuit. Published in 1989, *Echo of Lions* is a slice of history in novel form. Its focus is Joseph Cinque, who was captured in 1839 in what is now Sierra Leone, and brought to Cuba on the Spanish slaving ship *Amistad*. There Cinque led a revolt against the crew, and the newly freed Africans commandeered the ship and fled north. They finally were captured and imprisoned in New Haven, Connecticut. Charged with murder and piracy, Cinque became a rallying point for the abolitionists, especially when former president John Quincy Adams, who was now serving in Congress, took up his cause.

As there was not much literature readily available on the subject, Chase-Riboud spent several years researching the case, going into the papers of John Quincy Adams, examining the culture of Cinque's Mende tribe, poring over court transcripts, newspaper accounts, and diaries. Telling the story in the form of a novel allowed her to fabricate details she could not find or verify, and to create incidents and characters for dramatic purposes. For example, though there is no evidence Adams and Cinque ever met, she created a relationship between them, with Cinque influencing Adams's handling of the case.

The book was published to solid reviews and sold more than half a million copies around the world. Before publication no one less than Jacqueline Kennedy Onassis, a friend of the writer, asked Chase-Riboud if she would send a copy of her manuscript to Amblin' Entertainment. Chase-Riboud heard back from Kathleen Kennedy, one of Spielberg's top producers, requesting a meeting between the writer and Amblin' which took place in April 1988. It was a friendly meeting, but the feeling was that the material was perhaps better suited to a TV miniseries than to a feature film. When the book came out the following year, Chase-Riboud sent a copy to Amblin', but she heard nothing further from them.

Fast forward to 1996 when the author, now living in Paris, learned that the new DreamWorks studio was planning a production entitled *Amistad*. Executive producer Walter Parkes had been quoted as saying that Spielberg "was taken from the outset with the possibilities of telling an intimate story between two extraordinary men—an African slave and an ex-president of the United States—set against a historical backdrop." Chase-Riboud was not only upset, she had been down the path before. She had discovered that someone was writing a play about the subject of her first book, Sally Hemmings. She prevailed in federal court, with the playwright enjoined from publishing or selling the play until after he executed a licensing agreement with Chase-Riboud.

The complaint against DreamWorks was dramatic enough to be a script in its own right. The author hired Pierce O'Donnell, one of the top entertainment lawyers in California and the man who had successfully sued Paramount Pictures on behalf of Washington humor columnist Art Buchwald over plagiarism in their production of the comedy *Coming to America*. In the *Amistad* dispute, the pleadings began dramatically. "This case is about the original sin of American history—slavery," O'Donnell stated in his introduction to the complaint, not getting to the real case, that of copyright infringement, until a few pages later. He wielded a pen (or a word processor) with the dexterity of a stiletto, noting that *Echo of Lions* had become an archetypal novel of slavery, comparable to what Charles Dickens had written on the subject of child labor with *Oliver Twist*, what John Steinbeck had done for migrant workers with *The Grapes of Wrath*, and—now watch him twist the knife—what "Steven Spielberg's movie *Schindler's List* is becoming for the Jewish Holocaust."

Having shown that Spielberg and/or his agents had access to Chase-Riboud's manuscript, and also showing numerous similarities between their screenplay and *Echo of Lions*, O'Donnell dismissed what he entitled "DreamWorks' Incredible, Shifting Explanations" for the similarities between the two works. DreamWorks, of course, denied any connection with the novel, claiming its film was based on a different book on the same subject that had appeared in the 1980s. When it was pointed out that the only other book on the subject was a 1987 scholarly work entitled *Mutiny on the Amistad* by Howard Jones, which focused on legal and diplomatic issues rather than characters, another source was cited: the 1953 book *The Long Black Schooner* by Emma Stern. This, however, turned out to be a children's book, without much of the detail to be found in *Echo* and the movie script. A third source was then produced, *Black Mutiny* by William A. Owens, published in 1953. The complaint alleged that DreamWorks hadn't even acquired the rights to this last book until after Chase-Riboud began complaining. (In another twist to an already tangled situation, the rights to the Owens book had been optioned by actress Debbie Allen, who had long been interested in an *Amistad* film and would end up with a producer credit.)

Plagiarism suits are not unusual in Hollywood. Many complaints of "stolen ideas" are brought against movies after the fact. Some even have merit. Ideas do get stolen, whether by design or inadvertence, but there are also people ready to harp on the slightest similarity in the hope they will be paid off as a nuisance because that would be cheaper than going to court. But the weight of the facts and her legal representation made it clear that if Chase-Riboud's claim wasn't quite a slam dunk, this was no gadfly action either. This was serious business, particularly since Chase-Riboud wasn't asking only for money. She wanted an injunction that would prevent (or at least delay) the release of the film. If she succeeded, DreamWorks would have a prestige Steven Spielberg film that it couldn't show anyone, much less place in contention for an Oscar.

With the introduction of a formal complaint, DreamWorks brought out its own big guns, including lawyer Bert Fields, himself one of the major players in entertainment law. (Fields was also representing Jeffrey Katzenberg in his lawsuit for a share of the profits from his years at Disney.) Fields harped on the obvious Achilles' heel of the legal action, which was that the *Amistad* revolt was an historical event. "You can't own a piece of American history," said Fields. He also professed to be surprised that Chase-Riboud would prevent a wider audience from learning about this chapter in history, telling the *New York Times*, "The real sad thing is that this woman should be supporting this project and not trying to stop it to grab some money for herself."

If her suit had had no merit, Fields's charge of greed might have hit home, but on the facts presented it was fairly debatable that a valid claim existed. In either case, whether it was possible to copyright history or not, the lawsuit tied DreamWorks's publicity machine in knots. The film was set for a December 10 opening date. The court hearing on the injunction was scheduled for two days before, offering little time to appeal an adverse ruling.

In a sideshow to this, the Writers Guild of America, which arbitrates writers' credits on film, was hearing a dispute between DreamWorks and the original screenwriter, David Franzoni. DreamWorks had submitted a writing credit that would include not only Franzoni but also Steve Zaillian, who had adapted *Schindler's List* and had been brought in to do some work on the *Amistad* script. The studio also wanted to note that it was based on the 1953 Owens book. The Guild, after a dispute with Franzoni over whether he had ever read *Echo of Lions*, ended up giving him sole screenplay credit. In its decision, the Guild maintained that Franzoni had said at a September hearing that he had read the book. Franzoni and DreamWorks maintained this was an error in the Guild's transcript of the session. Their exceptions and the subsequent revision of the record occurred after Chase-Riboud's lawsuit had been filed.

"It's amazing. Their house of cards is crumbling," said attorney John Shaeffer, part of O'Donnell's firm and the team trying the case. "We can now see why they are focusing all their efforts on Barbara's credibility." Indeed, the new line was that she had stolen from other sources for her own book and was in no position to claim anyone had stolen from her.

DreamWorks dodged one bullet when the motion for a preliminary injunction was denied. The studio hailed this as a great victory. The film, which Spielberg was now calling one of the most important of his career, would be released on schedule, meaning it would be within the window to qualify for that year's Oscars. But the judge ruled that the rest of Chase-Riboud's complaint could proceed to trial, which meant that the suit for damages for the claimed infringement was very much alive.

Lawyers for both sides insisted that the case was in the bag and that they would shred the claims of the other side, but there was never to be a definitive ruling on the subject. In February 1998 the lawsuit was settled, and a confidentiality agreement prohibited the parties from discussing the terms of the settlement. Chase-Riboud issued a statement praising the film: "I think 'Amistad' is a splendid piece of work, and I applaud Mr. Spielberg for having the courage to make it."

Nonetheless the damage had been done. The lawsuit was settled just a day or two before the Oscar nominations were announced, and what had once been considered DreamWorks's entry into the awards sweepstakes received only four nominations. The biggest one was not for Spielberg's direction (which was snubbed) but for Anthony Hopkins's turn as John Quincy Adams. (He would lose the Supporting Actor award to *Good Will Hunting*'s Robin Williams.) Additional nominations came in for cinematography, dramatic score, and costume; all would go down before that year's Oscar juggernaut, *Titanic*.

DreamWorks publicity chief Terry Press did what she could to put a happy face on things, glibly telling the press, "Controversy helps because the public's consciousness and awareness of the movie goes up."

People may have been aware of the movie, but it didn't make them want to see it. *Amistad* took in an anemic $44 million at the box office and less than half that in worldwide grosses. Other than the settlement, if any, received by Chase-Riboud, only the publishers of William A. Owen's long-forgotten *Black Mutiny* seem to have benefited from the controversy. That book was put back in print in conjunction with the release of the film.

Three years after its founding, DreamWorks had little to show for its efforts.

5

Sideshows

IF IT IS REMEMBERED for anything at all, DreamWorks will be remembered as a movie studio. But that's not all it was nor all it was intended to be. From the start it aimed to have a strong animation unit, a full-fledged television division providing programming for the networks, cable, and syndication, and a music division where David Geffen would have an opportunity to show that lightning could indeed strike three times. There would also be a DreamWorks unit working on digital media both for the Internet and for release on CD ROM, which would combine Hollywood's creativity with the latest in technical wizardry.

DreamWorks's greatest success was its animation division, eventually spun off as a public company (and discussed in some detail in later chapters). The other parts of the company had their moments in the sun, some more than others, and a success or two to point at, yet in the end all failed to fulfill their promise. What went wrong in each case demonstrates not only how the DreamWorks team miscalculated but also how much the marketplace had changed. In many ways, DreamWorks would prove to be a vision whose time had already gone.

When Rupert Murdoch, Barry Diller, and Jamie Kellner launched the FOX television network in 1986, the world of American television was a very different place. There were only three networks: CBS, NBC, and ABC. An FCC regulation called the financial-interest syndication rule, or "fin/syn" for short, prohibited the owners of networks from having an ownership interest in the entertainment shows they aired. Cable television was an established but still growing phenomenon. There was no competition from DVDs or the Internet, and there were many recently created independent stations open to the idea of becoming affiliated with a brand-new network. The old guard realized it only in retrospect, but the time was ripe for an aggressive and deep-pocketed entity like FOX to come along and shake things up. For one thing, until the "fin/syn" rule finally was allowed to expire in November 1995, FOX was in the sweet position of being the only network that was part of a company that was also permitted to produce TV shows for itself and rival networks. This was because the FCC kept changing the definition of a network (how many hours broadcast nationally, how many broadcast in prime time) so that FOX wasn't—technically, at least—considered a network.

DreamWorks had no intention of buying a television network when it started setting up its TV division, and that put the studio at a disadvantage, as it soon discovered. Realizing that, as with movies, DreamWorks needed to establish operations not only for the production of its TV shows but also for their distribution, it hired Bob Jacquemin, former head of distribution for Buena Vista Television, part of the Disney empire. Jacquemin was one of the best in the business and wouldn't have to waste time introducing himself and making contacts. Everyone knew him. Recognizing that TV series could be turned around more quickly than feature films—and that the networks operated according to a calendar for buying shows that could not shift even for DreamWorks—the studio quickly began making deals. The emphasis was on stars, though one of the first arrangements announced was with Gary David Goldberg, the man behind the hit eighties sitcom *Family Ties*.

Early on DreamWorks focused on making deals that brought in a considerable investment in return for placements of the future product on the small screen. A joint venture with Capital Cities / ABC gave ABC first shot at DreamWorks series and had Spielberg salivating at the prospect of taking over the network's Saturday morning programming. He had been behind two animated series in the early nineties—*Tiny Toon Adventures* and *Animaniacs*—that had been popular with kids, attracted a cult audience of teens and adults, and had good responses from critics. The notion of Spielberg running Saturday morning for the network suggested a lot of young talent getting the freedom to break out of formula, as *Tiny Toon* and *Animaniacs* had. The overall deal had each side putting up $100 million for the production of all kinds of television programming over a seven-year period.

Then DreamWorks announced an exclusive deal with HBO to give the pay channel exclusive first runs of its movies after they'd completed their theatrical, home-video, and pay-per-view showings. HBO was said to benefit from the deal because it looked like it was about to lose future films from Paramount. Although this worked to DreamWorks's advantage, the reason Paramount was breaking with HBO should have set off alarm bells. Paramount had just been bought by Viacom, the media giant that would later merge with CBS. Viacom owned HBO's rival, Showtime. Thus it was to Viacom's advantage to have its Paramount films showing on its Showtime premium cable channel.

If that wasn't enough, the next news item was a comparative earthquake. Disney was buying ABC from Cap Cities. That was bad news for DreamWorks for two reasons. First, as an entertainment giant with a long track record of animation and family entertainment, Disney might respect Spielberg but certainly didn't need him to run *its* Saturday morning lineup. Second, Disney was Katzenberg's former employer, and he was engaged in an ugly lawsuit that pitted him against his old boss, Disney chairman Michael Eisner. It's not unheard of in Hollywood for parts of companies to be suing each other while other parts are in business together, but the Katzenberg/Eisner lawsuit was personal.

David Geffen tried to put the best face on it, telling the *New York Times*, "Michael Eisner is a very smart guy, very creative and now sitting on top of the most important media company in the world. If he takes care of those obligations to Jeffrey I'm happy to say let bygones be bygones." He added that if things didn't work out, they had the contractual option to walk away from the ABC deal.

Disney paid $19 billion to acquire ABC and had no intention of chasing DreamWorks away. But while DreamWorks shows would find slots on the ABC schedule (*Champs*, a sitcom from Gary David Goldberg to star Timothy Busfield, was announced as a midseason replacement in ABC's lineup), it was the end of any cozy relationship the two entities might have had in mind. Knowing what a blow this would be—particularly with Disney as purchaser—ABC executives had frantically tried to reach Katzenberg to inform him of the deal before it was made public. DreamWorks had already hired two former Disney animators, Gary Krigel and Bruce Canston, to run its TV animation unit, but with the exception of the short-lived *Father of the Pride* many years later, the unit was not to be.

The Disney acquisition of ABC changed things substantially, and it was a signal that the whole TV industry was changing. Fox and Disney now owned networks. Paramount had an interest in the weblet UPN, just getting under way, while Warners had its own network, the WB. Soon Paramount would merge with CBS, and in 2004 Universal and NBC would join forces (with General Electric holding 80 percent of the stock). Instead of entering the field as a major studio, DreamWorks was now coming in as a mere production company without its own television outlet.

Katzenberg put on his game face and said he looked forward to working with Disney: "For the last six months, the partnership with Cap Cities / ABC has been very successful and rewarding for us. I don't see any reason why we shouldn't be able to continue the relationship, but I think Disney has to decide what it wants out of this partnership."

What it wanted, apparently, were hit shows for prime time. With *Champs* set to go, ABC announced it would premiere in January 1996 in the favored Tuesday time slot currently held by *Coach*. The latter series would take a break while *Champs* had a chance to establish itself. It was a great slot for a launch, but after the initial sampling viewers didn't stick around, and the show quickly left the schedule.

Not until the fall did DreamWorks get its TV hit, also developed by Gary David Goldberg, but this time reuniting him with his *Family Ties* star Michael J. Fox. *Spin City* premiered in the fall of 1996, and it proved to be the right time for a sitcom that dabbled in politics in a way that didn't turn off younger viewers or alienate partisans of either side. It was set in the fictional administration of New York City mayor Randall M. Winston, Jr. As played by Barry

Bostwick, Mayor Winston was a bit absentminded but well intentioned. He came from inherited wealth and was so used to having things done for him that he understood the need to surround himself with good people. Chief among them was Deputy Mayor Mike Flaherty (Fox), who was the anchor for the show. Goldberg proceeded to surround Fox with such a rich cast of supporting characters that the series survived several cast changes, including the departure of Fox himself when he was diagnosed with Parkinson's disease and was replaced by Charlie Sheen in the final two seasons. *Spin City* was never a huge hit, but it scored solid ratings—ranking 17 out of the top 20 in its first season—and ran for six years. It pulled in young adult viewers and was able to hold on long enough to achieve the sitcom Holy Grail: syndication.

Unfortunately a studio producing TV series needs more than one hit show, and DreamWorks floundered trying to figure out how to repeat its success. *Ink* with Ted Danson and Mary Steenburgen and *Arsenio* with Arsenio Hall both had troubled starts. *Murphy Brown* creator Diane English was brought in to help *Ink*, which lasted a season on CBS, while series creator David Rosenthal clashed with Hall and ended up being dumped from his own series. It was canceled shortly thereafter. As a *U.S. News and World Report* survey of DreamWorks put it at the time, "Television has been the weakest link in the chain." The studio would eventually realize big money in the syndication of *Spin City* (some $2.5 to $3 million per episode), but that only helped defray the costs of the TV division's failures.

Any television production company has its ups and downs, and even the most successful operations turn out flop shows. What was different now was that the marketplace had changed significantly. NBC was interested in doing business with DreamWorks—but only if it could be a partner on the projects. DreamWorks pulled the plug on a couple of series in development when NBC demanded a financial interest in the shows. Instead of seeing this as an investment opportunity and a chance to share the risk—as it was doing under the ABC deal—DreamWorks balked. This was the future of network television, but DreamWorks couldn't see it. Ironically NBC would become home to the only other DreamWorks series to enjoy an extended run on broadcast television, the fast-paced *Las Vegas*. It had a strong and extremely attractive cast headed by James Caan and proved that lightweight eye candy didn't have to be stupid. By then Katzenberg was singing a different tune about co-production deals with the networks because he had very little choice: "The world has changed. You can stick your head in the sand and ignore that at your own peril. This is the new way to be in the TV business. . . . "

However much one might enjoy *Spin City* or *Las Vegas* or both, there was nothing extraordinary about either of them. They were slick, well-crafted entertainments that could have been produced by any other studio in Hollywood. When DreamWorks tried to do something different, it didn't last. *Undeclared*, a comedy set in a freshman college dorm, received some strong reviews but weak ratings. *Boomtown* was a crime drama coming at a time when crime dramas dominated the schedule, yet its fractured storytelling—examining a crime from multiple viewpoints—left viewers unsatisfied. *Father of the Pride* was an attempt to bring *Shrek*-style animation to TV, with John Goodman as the voice of the father of a family of lions working for Siegfried and Roy in Las Vegas. The show was gasping for life before the axe came down partway through its first season.

DreamWorks enjoyed a bit more success on cable. *Band of Brothers*, a well-received World War II miniseries, ran on HBO. It had Spielberg and Tom Hanks, fresh off their triumph of *Saving Private Ryan*, as executive producers, with Hanks also writing and directing some of the episodes. Steven Spielberg was also an executive producer of *Taken*, which was a blockbuster ratings event for the Sci-Fi Channel. Capitalizing on Spielberg's association with science-fiction themes, particularly *Close Encounters of the Third Kind*, it was heavily promoted as *Steven Spielberg Presents "Taken"*. The 2005 miniseries *Into the West* was savaged by negative reviews but pulled respectable numbers for TNT.

The problem with miniseries, though, is that these expensive productions were quickly consumed by television, leaving the hope that foreign and DVD sales might provide additional income. When *Band of Brothers* was released to rave reviews it was noted that, at an estimated $120 million, it was considered the most expensive television program in history.

DreamWorks teamed with Denis Leary for his FX series *Rescue Me*, but like other DreamWorks successes it was a mid-range hit. Critics and FX viewers would talk about *The Shield* and *Nip/Tuck* while Leary's saga of New York City firefighters was almost an afterthought. The television side of DreamWorks just couldn't generate a hit that impacted the pop culture the way *Saving Private Ryan* or *Shrek* would do on the movie side. Television, though, has several streams into the marketplace, and it was on the syndication side that the clearest picture of a company not quite sure why it was even in the television business emerged.

In the spring of 1996 Maury Povich, hosting his own syndicated daytime talk show produced by Paramount, shocked the industry by announcing he would leave the show when his contract was up in 1998 and move to DreamWorks. There he would do a new show co-anchored with his wife, the veteran newswoman Connie Chung. The series would focus on a single topic daily, and syndicated sales would target prime access—that early evening slot just before prime-time network fare begins. What's more, it would air live at 7:30 p.m. on the East Coast, going up against such reigning but tiring franchises as *Jeopardy* and *Entertainment Tonight*.

This announcement shook up the industry for a number of reasons. It's unusual to announce the launch of a new syndicated program two years in advance. Second, ABC and NBC stations in the major markets were already locked into long-term deals for other shows, which offered Dream-Works limited outlets for its ambitious launch. *Variety* speculated that CBS stations would be the likeliest home for such a series. Of course, by letting the cat out of the bag so early, DreamWorks gave CBS the advantage. The studio would need them much more than they might need any proposed Povich/Chung show.

The idea for the show originated not with Povich but with DreamWorks. Ken Solomon had been recruited from the FOX network, where he had become the head of distribution after starting out at Paramount as an intern in the early 1980s. (Solomon recalls delivering television ratings to Katzenberg at 6:30 in the morning, with Katzenberg already having been in his office for some time.) Although no one at DreamWorks had a title, Solomon was part of the amorphous television division, working with Bob Jacquemin, the Disney veteran.

They saw that the time was ripe for what they called a populist version of *Nightline*. Ratings were dropping for the traditional network newscasts, but "infotainment" remained a draw. Solomon knew Povich and felt he had great credibility with the audience. He also saw a real attraction in pairing him on air with Chung, who had had a falling out with CBS News. "We started talking about the ability to have a five-day-a-week news presence with two strong anchors of completely different points of view," said Solomon.

Povich and Chung's agent told the studio it could never come up with enough money to entice the two, but the DreamWorks team kept working on the model. One of them would be in the field, the other in the studio. One would do interviews, the other could lead a town-hall-style meeting. Solomon felt they had really come up with something, noting that this was before FOX News or NBC's *Dateline*. This might be an entirely new vehicle for news. What's more, the DreamWorks team pointed out to Povich and Chung that they could make far more money in syndication—as partners in the show—than they could on the networks or as mere employees.

In early 1996 the DreamWorks jet headed to New York on a mission to sew up the talent for not one but two big shows. Part of the team, including producer Gary David Goldberg, had a meeting with Michael J. Fox, hoping to persuade him to return to network television. The company was barely under way in terms of putting anything in production, but while one group was going to meet with Fox, the others were going to meet with Povich and Chung, hoping to pull off a coup. Katzenberg, in his "Golden Retriever" mode, was on the flight and considered both deals important. He divided his time between the two meetings.

The DreamWorks task force met with Povich and Chung in their home in the Dakota, the famous and luxurious Manhattan apartment building. Povich and Chung were impressed with the thoroughness of the presentation and finally said yes. Recalled Solomon, "We realized we had a chance to really change television at that very moment with something that no one was going to be able to say 'No' to. . . . We knew we were going to be a huge success with this thing."

Chung described the show as a "substantive news program," explaining, "We'll take whatever it is people are talking about around the water cooler that day and treat it in depth." Povich, who between *A Current Affair* and his talk show had a track record with syndicated infotainment, agreed that this represented something different. "My career has been so checkered in terms of the programs I've been involved with. This is going to represent an exciting new challenge for me."

In the farcical end to the day, Katzenberg was so pleased that he relaxed and continued chatting with Povich and Chung, seemingly oblivious to the fact that his television people were trying to catch the last flight out of New York to Denver so they could attend the Aspen Comedy Festival. Katzenberg was in no rush because he was taking the DreamWorks plane out of Teeterboro, not a commercial flight out of La Guardia. The group finally left, the TV executives heading to one of the limos while Katzenberg walked to the other. Solomon's group told the driver they must get to the heliport before the other car because they intended to take the helicopter for La Guardia before Katzenberg had a chance to countermand their orders. When they arrived, Gary David Goldberg was waiting, gleeful that he had persuaded Fox to do *Spin City*. The executives raced right by, boarded the helicopter, and were off to La Guardia where they made their connecting flight.

"We figured since we had gotten the 'get' it was a good career bet that he wasn't going to fire us for taking his helicopter. Besides, his plane will wait and ours won't," said Solomon, who proved to be right.

They were euphoric, but a year later things weren't looking so good. Given the limited choices it had, DreamWorks was now saying it would offer the show for "fringe access," which meant a time slot or two farther away from prime time. There was some talk of getting the FOX group of stations to pick up the show to run after their local 10 p.m. newscasts, as FOX didn't run network shows in the final hour of prime time. CBS was still the ideal fit, but with the launch more than a year away, the network could bide its time and see what else was in the marketplace before making a commitment to DreamWorks.

Some top stations signed on. DreamWorks sold the show to ratings leaders in Hartford and Minneapolis, but that's not how success is measured in launching a new syndicated show. One needs strong outlets in the top markets like New York, Los Angeles, and Chicago or you're simply not playing in the big leagues. At NATPE, the television program executives convention and market, DreamWorks brought in Povich and Chung to pitch the show and wow the stations. It began lining up top producers in television news to work on the show. It was making it clear that whatever it took, DreamWorks meant business.

CBS had just merged with radio giant Infinity Broadcasting, and Infinity executive Mel Karmazin was emerging in the spring of 1997 as the person in charge of CBS's radio and television properties. While that was being sorted out, CBS was not concentrating on a show that wouldn't launch until September 1998. Povich, who still had another year on his contract at Paramount, where there was now considerable tension, was growing nervous. He talked about continuing his talk show at DreamWorks, at least for the end of its run at the stations, at no additional cost to DreamWorks. Katzenberg nixed the idea. The focus was on locking down a deal with the CBS stations. If DreamWorks had that, it would have a great launch and nothing else would matter.

Solomon told Katzenberg to be patient. Karmazin would have to get his bearings, but would then realize that CBS's aging King World shows (*Jeopardy*, *Wheel of Fortune*) could be replaced. "Then we'll get the prime-time access period," Solomon said, convinced it was the only logical outcome. He and Bob Jacquemin even made a pitch to Roger King, the owner of King World, to pull his shows and come in on the Povich/Chung deal. King was open to the offer but wanted in on DreamWorks prime-time offerings as well, and they couldn't come to terms.

One year before the scheduled launch of the Povich/Chung show, DreamWorks had signed up stations covering 30 to 40 percent of the country, which was not yet enough but was way ahead of the game for a syndicated show at that stage. If it could close the deal for the CBS-owned stations it would cover 80 percent of the country and be in all the top markets. Povich continued to worry it wouldn't come off and insisted that the deal include a talk show for him so he would be covered either way. For some reason, though, in the end it was Katzenberg who got cold feet.

While his executives kept telling him to hang in there, that CBS would make the deal, Katzenberg became convinced that CBS would never do it and that the show would either never launch or launch so weakly that it would fail. So instead of going ahead with what might have been an innovative news program and a bold stake in television for DreamWorks, the studio suddenly killed the deal. Povich and Chung were released from their commitments and, out of a sense of obligation for pulling him away from his deal at Paramount, Solomon connected Povich with Greg Meidel, a former colleague at FOX who was now at Universal, which is where Povich ended up. Solomon soon followed suit, leaving DreamWorks for a position at Universal.

There's an ironic punch line to the story. Several months later Solomon was introduced to Karmazin. Solomon was now president of Universal Television, and he said, "Mel, I actually want to thank you for my job. I wouldn't have my job if it wasn't for you." Karmazin asked him to explain. "Well, I had a show that I was convinced you were going to buy, but my boss wouldn't wait for you to get into the position and make the decision. So I got offered this and I took it."

Karmazin asked him what show, and Solomon described the proposed Povich/Chung program. According to Solomon, Karmazin heard this and said, "I would have bought that show in a second." Instead, because Dream-Works canceled the project, CBS went ahead with a revived version of the old game-show war-horse *Hollywood Squares*.

By the fall of 1998, with *Spin City* doing well but no Povich/Chung show and little else to show for its TV operations, DreamWorks was already reducing expectations. Asked about TV operations, Geffen was dismissive: "It's not one of our main businesses."

If any business should have come naturally to DreamWorks after movies, it was music. David Geffen had become wealthy beyond his dreams from his two record labels, and now he was launching a third.

He was delayed a few months before he could get to work on the new DreamWorks Records because his deal with MCA, which had bought out Geffen Records, obligated him through April 1995. According to Geffen's biographer, Tom King, Geffen did not feel the need to be fully involved in the DreamWorks start-up. He rarely went to his office (located in Spielberg's Amblin' Entertainment complex at Universal), though he stayed in touch with both Katzenberg and Spielberg throughout the day.

DreamWorks Records made its first major news by signing rock star George Michael, who had had a falling out with Sony, where he had his current deal. There was a problem, though, in getting Michael away from Sony, even though he wanted to leave. It was messy enough that it was likely to end up in court. Ever the dealmaker, Geffen arranged for a large settlement of Michael's contract with Sony (estimates were in the $6 million range), which was a pretty steep price considering that none of that included payments to Michaels, which were a separate item. The deal was so pricey that it might not be worth it unless Michael's new album was a huge hit—but Geffen got what he wanted out of it. The deal put his new label on the map.

Geffen had little interest in the day-to-day affairs of the music operation and put together a team he could trust to run the label. The key appointment was that of recording industry veteran Mo Ostin, with whom Geffen had a long relationship, not always a good one. Ostin had been pushed out at Warner Bros. after more than three decades there, and such was his reputation that everyone else wanted him. In spite of a rocky history with Geffen, he decided that DreamWorks offered him the best deal. In October 1995 Ostin came on board, joined by his son Michael and Lenny Waronker, current president of Warner Bros. Records. Ostin boasted that shifting over to a smaller operation would be liberating: "We won't have the baggage that you have at some of the bigger corporations. If we focus on less artists and less releases, we're gonna have a much better success ratio."

Given this star talent on the business side, DreamWorks Records elicited high expectations. Larry Tisch, CEO of CBS, told *Fortune* magazine, "I think records could well end up the most valuable part of the company." Rarely noted was that Geffen would have little to do with actually running the operation. "Mo Ostin is the head of the music company," Geffen insisted, even though DreamWorks's rule of no titles for anyone applied here as well. "I'm his partner. I'll help when I can."

As with the movie and TV sides, the trade press was buzzing about the music start-up news and hirings, but eventually they wanted to see what sort of product the company turned out. Michael's first new album in several years, *Older*, did not achieve the platinum status in sales that his earlier releases had enjoyed. Some thought Michael past his prime, and that made DreamWorks appear to be out of touch. For his part, Michael complained that DreamWorks did not handle the album properly. The label had better luck with the original-cast album for the hit Broadway show *Rent*, a retelling of the opera *La Bohème* in contemporary Manhattan. It also enjoyed some success with the release of a comedy album by the hot comic Chris Rock.

The problem was that DreamWorks Records was not about to make its reputation with show tunes or stand-up comedy, no matter how cutting edge. Observers noted that the label was failing to define itself. Ostin professed not to be concerned. "We're trying to create a haven for artists," said Ostin. "We're not concerned about trends. If bubblegum happens to be the moment, that's not what we're going to sign. But we'll make money. We did that in a previous incarnation, and it will happen again."

All stops were pulled out for the release of the long-awaited animated feature *Prince of Egypt*. DreamWorks Records announced it would release three different CDs in connection with the film. The soundtrack album of Stephen Schwartz's original song score would also feature selections from Hans Zimmer's orchestral score and some alternate pop versions of a few songs, including a duet performed by Whitney Houston and Mariah Carey. Then there would be two albums "inspired by" the movie, one a country album and the other gospel and soul. The simultaneous release of three different albums linked to one movie would be a real test of the music division's marketing muscle, and it went all out. A special was prepared with NBC, "When You Believe: Music from *The Prince of Egypt*." It was Katzenberg who insisted the movie be treated as an event rather than simply a merchandising opportunity. Said Ostin, "Because of the film's subject matter, DreamWorks was very careful not to do things that were overtly commercial."

Showing a marketing savvy that would pay off for subsequent animated releases, DreamWorks arranged to have big displays at the Virgin Megastores, which would showcase all three CDs connected to the film. Unfortunately the Virgin Megastore in Orlando, Florida, was located at Disney World, and the Disney Company had the right in its lease to veto major promotions for rival productions. The fact that Katzenberg's lawsuit against Disney was coming to a head probably didn't help matters.

"It's part of their lease. We have no recourse," admitted DreamWorks sales executive Joyce Castagnola.

By 2001 the movie side of DreamWorks was going great guns, with *Saving Private Ryan*, *American Beauty*, *Gladiator*, and *Shrek* among its hits. The music label, though, remained in the shadows. *Billboard* reported that a few cuts from various albums were hitting the charts, with Lifehouse's "Hanging by a Moment" not only poised to top the chart but also about to become the first DreamWorks track to be on the charts for twenty weeks. The music division would release eighteen albums that year, a high for the label but considered low for the competition.

Ultimately for DreamWorks, music would turn out to be "not one of our main businesses," just as television had. The investment was going into film and feature animation, and despite the prediction of CBS's Larry Tisch, the music side of DreamWorks wasn't where the action was. Ironically he did turn out to be right in the sense of music bringing money into the company. In October 2004 the company sold DreamWorks Records to Universal Music Group for $100 million. A month later DreamWorks Music Publishing, which held the rights to the music itself as opposed to the recordings, was sold to Dimensional Associates for another $40 to 50 million. The DreamWorks catalog was estimated at some seven thousand songs.

As the company celebrated its tenth anniversary, it was out of the music business altogether.

For a company that would help revolutionize animation through the use of computer technology, the world of interactive computer games and websites should have been the area where the rest of the industry looked to DreamWorks to see how it was done. Instead, and despite all the expertise at its command, the company treated this side of the business as an afterthought. A good idea would come up, a new business would be announced—and then some time later it would be quietly sold off or shut down.

In their initial business plan the troika foresaw investing $75 million in interactive games and software by 2000. This compared with $190 million in television, $25 million in music, $200 million in animation, and a whopping $800 million in feature films. To be decided was whether Dream-Works should purchase an existing game and software company, start a new one, or go into a joint venture. Spielberg was already an investor in a software company called Knowledge Adventure, but it fell by the wayside when Bill Gates and the troika came to terms. (Some five titles had been developed through Spielberg's involvement with Knowledge Adventure, the last of them going out in 1996.) Instead they concentrated on the newly formed Dream-Works Interactive, with DreamWorks and Microsoft each putting up $15 million for the start-up. It expected to hire about seventy-five employees at the time of the announcement in March 1995, and Microsoft would handle distribution of the DreamWorks Interactive products.

"We will release between three and five titles by Christmas of 1996, and around a dozen titles in 1997," boldly predicted Leslie Koch, a Microsoft manager who was part of the team setting up the unit. The games would feature lots of adventures, some of them based on DreamWorks's lineup of movies and TV shows, but also original games. Meanwhile Microsoft would continue to develop its own interactive games.

Plans were expansive. Not only would there be the usual games that the purchaser installed on a home computer;

DreamWorks Interactive would also develop multiplayer on-line games. Slowly some releases appeared. A game based on the *Goosebumps* series of kid-oriented horror novels did well, as did one based on Spielberg's non-DreamWorks movie *The Lost World: Jurassic Park*.

By contrast, DreamWorks had no idea how to use the world of the Internet to promote its new movies on-line. *Saving Private Ryan* had no web promotion. Its first few kid-oriented films—*Mousehunt*, *Paulie*, and *Small Soldiers*—were farmed out to the FreeZone website, a subsidiary of a Canadian publisher, which focused on younger Internet surfers. It was a clever way to promote the films to the target audience, but why couldn't it have been done in house? "They've got great ideas, the kinds of things I couldn't do on my own because I don't have the staff," admitted Michael Vollman, DreamWorks's head of field promotions.

By 2000 it was obvious that while DreamWorks was greatly interested in the digital side of moviemaking, the sideline of interactive games was neither sustaining itself nor worth further investment. A *Los Angeles Business Journal* report quoted an industry analyst: "DreamWorks hasn't hit the out-of-the-ball-park success it had hoped to have by now, and is still very much a small boutique shop." A spokesman for DreamWorks Interactive claimed it was profitable, and some of its recent releases had been well reviewed, but DreamWorks had clearly moved on. In 2000 the division was sold off to Electronic Arts, a major publisher in the video game field. Instead of focusing on games, DreamWorks decided that the company's digital future would be in a different direction. It bought Pacific Data Images, where DreamWorks already had an ownership interest. Pacific's specialty was computer-animated effects for the movies.

If DreamWorks was giving up on computer games it was only because, after all, the real future of interactivity was on the Internet, and DreamWorks was preparing to launch a co-venture with Ron Howard and Brian Grazer's Imagine Entertainment. It would be called Pop.com and would, they all hoped, become the hottest movie site on the web. Katzenberg compared it to the explosion of music videos in the early eighties leading to the creation of MTV: "This is an emerging and evolving new format. . . . We believe we are at that time and moment now for the Internet."

Word first appeared in the fall of 1999 that DreamWorks and Imagine would collaborate on this new website. It wasn't quite clear what was being promised—perhaps trailers, original short films, message boards, chat rooms—but it would launch in the spring of 2000. Spring came and went, and in July the word was that it would now launch in the fall. The buzz was positive. The trade journal *Inter@ctive Week* gushed, "Pop's launch is among the signs that Tinsel Town is starting to embrace the medium."

People were hired, films were commissioned, and things were humming along, though it wasn't quite clear where exactly they were going. There would be an office party on Friday afternoons complete with a drinks cart. People would socialize, and they'd view the latest acquisitions for the site—shorts that DreamWorks paid $10,000 to $20,000 to acquire. Ron Howard had done a series of animated shorts imagining the dreams of famous people (including himself and Spielberg). Steve Martin did a short in which he went out on a blind date with Claudia Schiffer, and another about his imagined life if he had married Gwyneth Paltrow. Mike Myers played a goofy Canadian wandering around Hollywood. Little of this would ever see the light of day.

Rumors soon began circulating that Pop.com would never be launched. When a story to that effect appeared in the *Los Angeles Times*, Katzenberg appeared at Pop.com's offices to calm the troops. Tim Doyle was there as part of a small group of independent contractors who were working on DreamWorks web projects. He recalled the day Katzenberg came to tell them that the rumors were wrong. "Jeffrey came over and hit a piñata and had a rally. Everyone was attacking the *L.A. Times*. There were stickers and all this other stuff. It was kind of kooky."

Then, abruptly, without ever having launched, Pop.com was finished. Over the Labor Day weekend of 2000, Dream-Works notified some ninety employees that their services for Pop.com would no longer be necessary. People reportedly walked off with equipment, and eventually guards were posted. There were also stories of the operation's legal department files suddenly vanishing. According to one account, some of the acquisitions people supposedly destroyed records of deals so that the filmmakers could retrieve their films from DreamWorks without having to negotiate.

Doyle didn't witness any such destruction, but he could confirm part of the story: "There were times when I know one of the business affairs people was expecting to find a deal that she knew had been negotiated and had signed off on, and it wasn't there. It happened multiple times."

DreamWorks would thereafter use the Internet as a marketing tool, with websites established for certain movies, but the effort wasn't taken seriously. The biggest innovation may have been the "BagelCam." When Spielberg was shooting *A.I.* he allowed the people running the website for DreamWorks to set up a camera at the craft services truck, where cast and crew would come for coffee or food. There was no sound, but the camera stayed live for several days. Spielberg would come over and wave, sometimes holding up a sign. Since this was while the film was in production, there was no full promotional website for the movie. Spielberg did it again during the shooting of *Minority Report*.

According to Doyle, "The marketing people are loath to commit to anything. It's difficult because they don't want to put themselves out there. In these cases it was because Spielberg was behind it and was interested in doing it. He wanted to innovate and do something interesting."

Spielberg rarely appeared among the people trying to set up Pop.com, and Geffen even less. Katzenberg was the member of the troika they saw most often and, in the end, he treated it like he did the Maury Povich / Connie Chung venture: he pulled the plug before it even launched. This wasn't an area where they intended to take big risks. An attempt to merge Pop.com with—or even sell out to—the short-film websites iFilms or AtomFilms fizzled. Mark Hulett, chief marketing officer for AtomFilms, claimed that the asking price to buy out Pop.com was simply too high. In the end, DreamWorks decided to use the Counting-Down.com site that Doyle had co-founded (originally to "count down" the days until *Titanic* was released) and that it had acquired to maintain its toehold on the web. It continues today as a fan-run movie site.

Like the Playa Vista studio, albeit on a small scale, Pop.com remains an example of DreamWorks dreaming big yet finally losing its nerve. It may simply be that the principals had no idea what they were getting into, but went ahead anyway. "You can't take existing models and port them over to a new-media venture," said Hulett.

DreamWorks's weak record in television, music, and high tech suggests that the Dream Team was going through the motions because that's what modern full-service studios were supposed to be doing. It became obvious that what they seemed to know best—or at least most wanted to do— was make movies. For a few years at least, it was in feature films that DreamWorks would show the rest of Hollywood how it could be done.

6

The Private and
the Prince

FOR A FEW YEARS DreamWorks rode high with movie audiences. Not every film clicked, but any tally of important films each year from 1998 through 2001 would include at least one DreamWorks release, perhaps more, and often they would be at the top of the list. Having survived the slings and arrows directed at its initial releases, Dream-Works was now ready to enter the fray fully. The good times began, of all places, on the beaches of Normandy.

The summer of 1998 got under way with the good news of a strong opening for *Deep Impact*, the first of two "giant meteors heading toward Earth" movies scheduled for release. Although it was overshadowed by the blockbuster *Armageddon*, it did respectable business. The only drawback was that while DreamWorks made money on the deal (the film grossed more than $200 million worldwide), it didn't really get the credit. The fishing boy on the crescent moon logo might pop up on screen, but the film was a co-production with Paramount, and it was Paramount that handled the domestic release. That, and the disappointing *Small Soldiers* (a comedy about killer toys that was too scary for young kids and too goofy for older ones), would soon be forgotten. The summer of 1998 was the summer of *Saving Private Ryan*.

After the disappointment and controversy over *Amistad*, Steven Spielberg had to hit one out of the ballpark for the home team, and that he did. *Saving Private Ryan* was not only the summer's top-grossing film, it was the biggest hit of the year, the favorite for the Oscars, and, perhaps more than that, a genuine—and positive—news event. It was a year when America was ready to look back at the World War II generation, which had saved the world more than half a century before, and give them their due before it was too late. Later that year Tom Brokaw's best-selling book *The Greatest Generation* tapped into that same reservoir, and the film and the book could be seen as reinforcing each other well into the next year.

The story of the movie was a deceptively simple one. After a harrowing re-creation of the D-day landing on Omaha Beach (a sequence that earned the film an R rating, only the third in Spielberg's career), we get to meet Captain John Miller (Tom Hanks) and his troops. Miller is given an assignment that is both understandable and frustrating. Private James Ryan (Matt Damon) is one of four brothers fighting in the war. His siblings have all died in combat, and the army has decided that the surviving son must be found and returned home. Miller and several soldiers are sent out to locate and retrieve Ryan. Private Richard Reiben (Edward Burns) sums up the dilemma of the movie when he asks Miller, "What's the sense in risking eight guys to save one?"

For the film Spielberg and his team assembled a great cast of young actors. In addition to Damon (who would win the Oscar for co-writing *Good Will Hunting* by the time *Ryan* was released) and Burns, there were also Barry Pepper, Adam Goldberg, Giovanni Ribisi, and Vin Diesel. Tom Sizemore was the tough-as-nails sergeant who was still sentimental enough to collect a bit of soil as a keepsake from the D-day invasion.

Then there was Hanks. After a start in goofy comedy roles in the eighties like TV's *Bosom Bodies* and the mermaid romance *Splash*, Hanks had become a major leading man. In films like *Sleepless in Seattle*, *Philadelphia*, and *Apollo 13*, he became an American everyman character, a regular guy tested in extraordinary circumstances. Even in *Forrest Gump* he played someone who could rely on audience support from the beginning. Critics compared him to Spencer Tracy and Jimmy Stewart, and they were not far off the mark. Hanks had developed his own style, learning how to underplay to great effect. One of the running jokes in *Saving Private Ryan* concerns Miller's men wondering what this serious and determined officer had done in civilian life. When it is finally revealed that he had been a schoolteacher, we see that he is no more a professional warrior than they. They have all been called upon to rise to the occasion in fighting for their country.

The actors spent several days camping in the woods in their uniform and gear, learning from the film's technical adviser, retired Marine captain Dale Dye, what it was like to be in combat. Hanks said it helped prepare them for their roles, simply having to keep on the move while carrying all the equipment. "We're essentially playing guys who are tired and miserable and want to go home," he noted. "Great physical demands are being made of them constantly."

Over the movie's nearly three-hour running time, Miller and his men encounter snipers and refugees, moments of violence and moments of rest. In the end Ryan is saved at terrible cost—as Reiben said, the math never did make sense—and in the patented mawkish and sentimental style that Spielberg favored and audiences loved, the film ends with the tear-stained veteran Ryan in the present day remembering those who died so that he might live. The music swells, the flags wave, and Spielberg delivers an honest-to-goodness box office hit for DreamWorks. Although there was a co-production deal with Paramount, as with *Deep Impact*, this time that lucky flip of a coin won DreamWorks the domestic release rights. They might have to share receipts, but the bragging rights were all theirs.

DreamWorks was taking no chances on this release. The film was set to open in late July, taking advantage of the cycle of the film calendar. From Memorial Day weekend to the Fourth of July, the summer's big guns are fired. Increasingly the opening salvos have been occurring in early May. Late July meant the film was positioned after audiences had been exposed to the blockbusters—potential and real. If it clicked it could play into the fall when the more adult films (read: Oscar contenders) were released.

Publicist Terry Press, a Disney veteran who engineered the campaign that won *Beauty and the Beast* the first Best Picture Oscar nomination for an animated film, positioned *Saving Private Ryan* as the serious grown-up film of the summer. Spielberg, Hanks, Damon, and the historian Stephen E. Ambrose—whose books inspired the film and who would later work on the Spielberg/Hanks miniseries *Band of Brothers*—went on a five-city tour to do interviews and promote the movie.

It was a tough sell. *Saving Private Ryan* had graphic violence, it was long, and it was about events that had occurred before much of the younger summer movie audience was born. "One of the best things we have going for it since the movie was cast is that Matt Damon became Matt Damon," said Press, happy to take advantage of his *Good Will Hunting* stardom and Oscar even if it occurred after *Ryan* had finished shooting.

The film went out in wide release, but a glitch at Technicolor caused a few hundred prints to be routed to the wrong theaters. As a result a theater in East Hampton on Long Island didn't have a print for the opening show. Ironically, it was the theater near Spielberg's summer home. If it bothered Spielberg, the annoyance couldn't have lasted long. The reviews were some of the best of his career, and very nearly unanimous. Writing in *Newsweek*, David Ansen had some problem with the framing device set in the present-day cemetery, but then dismissed it: "[T]he truth is, this movie so wiped me out I have little taste for quibbling. When you emerge from Spielberg's cauldron, the world doesn't look quite the same." Discussing the D-day battle scenes, Richard Schickel wrote in *Time* that they constituted "quite possibly the greatest combat sequence ever made." Janet Maslin in the *New York Times* did him one better, calling it "the finest war movie of our time."

It was that rare sort of movie that instantly became part of the culture. Sales of Ambrose's war histories reportedly rose, and travel agents noted new interest in tours of World War II battle sites. Pundits discussed what the popularity of the film meant while the Veterans Administration arranged for counselors to be available for aging ex-military men, now in their seventies, if seeing the film brought back a flood of hard memories to those who had fought in the war. *Variety* critic Todd McCarthy noted that the film appealed to those who had lived through the war but also to younger viewers who could relate to the young soldiers around their age and see what they had to go through. Wrote McCarthy, "Hardly a day has gone by without one columnist or another weighing in on the film's import, with some having gone so far as to suggest that it is only with *Private Ryan* that the lingering guilt and cynicism left behind by the Vietnam War has been wiped clean. How one judges this sort of thing is beyond me, but the fact that the film is being discussed in these terms indicates the depth of its impact."

Finally DreamWorks was on the map with a film of its own, even if it was a co-production with Paramount. When it won its expected slew of Oscars, it would be DreamWorks that got the glory. First, though, even before its long-awaited prestige animated musical based on the biblical book of Exodus, DreamWorks had a funny little computerized cartoon about ants.

With Spielberg—and, more particularly, his Amblin' producers Walter Parkes and Laurie MacDonald—calling the shots on DreamWorks live-action films, Katzenberg's domain had become animation. Of course with no titles at the studio, everyone consulted with everyone else, but everyone also knew who was really responsible for what. Katzenberg remained the one member of the troika who had something to prove. In spite of his impressive track record he had been ousted from Disney instead of getting the promotion he felt was his due. When he filed suit against Disney, he claimed at least $250 million as his share of profits for projects he had shepherded through production. Katzenberg made it clear where his loyalties were: "For ten years I lived and breathed the Walt Disney Company and I am proud of what we accomplished during that time. In the meantime I'm focusing on the future of DreamWorks."

It would be a very unpleasant lawsuit. Disney claimed that Katzenberg's contract contained a waiver of any claims on future profits or bonuses once he left the company. His attorney Bert Fields blasted the Disney position. "Katzenberg would have to be incompetent or insane to make the contract they claim he made, and Katzenberg is neither." Katzenberg would eventually prevail, but the Dream-Works/Disney competition seemed to persist. Disney was known for aggressively undercutting the competition, particularly when rival studios tried to move into their animation and family entertainment territory. When DreamWorks announced that its prestige holiday release *Prince of Egypt* would open on December 18, 1998, Disney scheduled its remake of the giant-ape family adventure *Mighty Joe Young* to open on the same date. *Variety* quoted an "insider" at Disney saying this was no mere coincidence. "I wish we didn't feel compelled to pussyfoot. We're competitive, just like Coke and Pepsi, and historically we've pulled out the stops to protect our turf." When Twentieth Century Fox released the animated *Anastasia* in November 1997, it found itself up against not only a re-release of Disney's animated hit *The Little Mermaid* but also the live-action remake *Flubber* with Robin Williams.

It was within this context that DreamWorks released its first cartoon feature, the computer-animated *Antz*. Later overshadowed by the box office smash *Shrek*, *Antz* set the stage for DreamWorks breaking from the Disney model. Although *Prince of Egypt* and several other DreamWorks animated releases would be done in traditional hand-drawn cel animation, *Antz* was the first time most moviegoers would see a computer-animated film that wasn't from Pixar, which had scored a big hit with *Toy Story* (1995), released through Disney under a long-term deal. In *Antz* the voice cast was part of the draw. Disney had long used celebrity voice casts, but its promotion centered on the film, not the actors. For *Antz* the advance publicity hyped the fact that this was the first cartoon to have Woody Allen in a featured role, as well as Sylvester Stallone, Sharon Stone, Gene Hackman, Anne Bancroft, Danny Glover, and Christopher Walken, among others. The hook of Woody Allen as a cartoon voice was noted; later the *Shrek* marketing campaign would emphasize its starring voice cast from the start.

Antz demonstrated that moviegoers weren't put off by computer animation, and that *Toy Story* was not a fluke. The animation for *Antz* was done by Pacific Data Images (PDI), a company in which DreamWorks decided, in 1996, to invest a 40 percent share. PDI had done some special-effects work on *The Peacemaker*, but with the new Dream-Works money—and the assignment to do much of the work on *Antz*—it expanded from 90 employees to 260.

There was rather pointed speculation in some quarters that *Antz* had been rushed into production by Katzenberg knowing that Pixar's next film, *A Bug's Life*, was being made before he left Disney. Katzenberg denied it, but Pixar's John Lasseter, who had directed *Toy Story* and was now doing *A Bug's Life*, was furious. "We were about a year and a half into our movie when we heard the news. My reaction was 'Why? Why would Jeffrey do that?'"

The real issue, though, was the film's release date. Katzenberg engaged in a game of "chicken" with Disney. *Antz* was announced as a March 1999 release. Disney then put *A Bug's Life* on the calendar for Thanksgiving 1998. In June Katzenberg moved *Antz* to an early October release, seven weeks before *A Bug's Life*. DreamWorks denied reports that it had drawn up two release schedules, one indicating *Antz* would not be finished until early 1999, the other revealing the October target. A DreamWorks animator who preferred to remain anonymous said, "It was *Mission: Impossible* time. They planned it like the Allies planned Normandy."

Indeed, this was not the only head-to-head battle with Disney animation. Already in production at DreamWorks was *The Road to El Dorado*, an animated adventure about a search for a city of gold during the sixteenth century. It would come out in March 2000. Disney's Inca-themed *The Emperor's New Groove* would be pushed back to December 2000. Although the ultimate test for the films would be their reception at the box office, this sort of gamesmanship showed that DreamWorks would not roll over for Disney. Carl Rosendahl, the president of PDI, downplayed the *Antz/Bug's Life* competition, calling the release of two computer-animated insect movies inside of two months a mere "coincidence."

For all the jockeying for position, the real issue was whether DreamWorks would succeed where so many other companies—most recently Warner Bros. and Twentieth Century Fox—had failed. Wrote *Variety* film critic Todd McCarthy, "No company has yet cracked Disney hegemony in the animation field, and it will be interesting to see how the latest chapter in the war plays out."

Antz made $90 million in domestic box office and an additional $80 million overseas, making it one of the most successful non-Disney animated films to date. The previous record holder had been the 1996 *Beavis and Butt-head Do America*, based on the MTV series, which took in only $63 million domestically (and a paltry $17 million overseas). When *A Bug's Life* appeared, it turned out to be much more family friendly than *Antz* and consequently was a much, much bigger hit. *Bug's Life* totaled more than $350 million in worldwide box office. Disney won the box office battle, but DreamWorks had shown it knew how to play the game. It still had the big gun of *Prince of Egypt*. And PDI had already begun work on DreamWorks's next computer-animated project, a film entitled *Shrek*.

Prince of Egypt was DreamWorks's prestige holiday film release. Long touted as its important entry in the animation sweepstakes, the film adapted the Disney style to a very un-Disney subject: the biblical story of Moses and the Exodus. The detailed animation was serious, yet creative. In one sequence the slaying of the Israelite firstborn was shown by having hieroglyphic images come to life. Celebrity voices were used again, but in the Disney style: you'd have to check the credits to see that the voices in *Prince of Egypt* included Val Kilmer (as Moses), Ralph Fiennes, Michelle Pfeiffer, Sandra Bullock, Jeff Goldblum, Patrick Stewart, Helen Mirren, Steve Martin, Martin Short, and Danny Glover. The star of the movie was not Val Kilmer, or even Moses. It was Jeffrey Katzenberg. This was to be the movie that would show he could produce great animated movies outside of Disney.

Marc Lumer was an animation artist working at DreamWorks at the time, working on designs and backgrounds on both *Prince of Egypt* and *Road to El Dorado*. Lumer found himself meeting once or twice a week with Katzenberg, who took a hands-on approach to the film. "Every drawing we did was submitted to him. The storyboards were pitched to him," recalled Lumer, who had previously worked on animation productions at Warner Bros. that were being produced by Spielberg. Lumer found the contrast between the two men striking. "[Spielberg] would seldom show on the animation shows he produced. He'd shake some hands, comment on drawings and boards. We'd get memos asking us not to request autographs," he said of the Warners experience. "At DreamWorks, Spielberg would show up a little more often in the animation department, but it was Jeffrey Katzenberg [who was always around]. He was like one of the workers there."

Katzenberg was more concerned with development than production. Once the film was actually shooting, the workers dealt more often and directly with the producers and directors. Katzenberg would help develop the style of the film, going into details as to the look of the buildings and even the shapes of the characters. "He was really working as a moviemaker," said Lumer.

Simon Wells, one of three directors on *Prince of Egypt*, recalled going into his first meeting with Katzenberg. "Jeffrey was clutching this book of sketches by the nineteenth-century illustrator Gustave Doré. He said he wanted the movie to have Doré's symmetry and lighting, Claude Monet's painting style and color, and David Lean's epic cinematography, like in *Lawrence of Arabia*. We almost fell on the floor." By the time the film was near release, Wells was taking it equally seriously, telling an interviewer that he no longer considered it simply an animated movie but "a film that happens to be drawn."

Along with that feeling of doing something new and different was the sense—among the animators at any rate—that they were about to beat Disney. Katzenberg was not the only Disney veteran at the new studio. Terry Press, chief of publicity, had been at Disney. So had Ann Daly, head of the feature animation division. Right from the start there had been rumors that Katzenberg was "raiding" the Disney animation department for talent, including a report that since his contract at Disney barred him from actively recruiting he intended to take a hotel room in Orlando and get the word out that he was available for visits from disgruntled members of Disney's Florida animation unit. Katzenberg's office denied this, as did Disney. A spokesman for Disney confirmed only one "major animator" leaving the studio for DreamWorks and blamed the reports of Disney animators jumping ship on Katzenberg: "Jeffrey's got his publicity machine in place, and that's the source of most of the rumors."

The competition played out in a number of ways. *Prince of Egypt* was an attempt not merely to make a financially successful animated picture but one that would rival Disney's best films in importance. The selection of subject matter showed that. Here was a well-known biblical story that had been famously put on film by Cecil B. DeMille as *The Ten Commandments*, the 1956 blockbuster with Charlton Heston that still had regular television airings but was showing its age. Since this was the Bible, the DreamWorks crew had to make sure its film did not give needless offense. The last thing Katzenberg wanted was controversy, no matter how hard Press had tried to spin the *Amistad* imbroglio. No detail of *Prince of Egypt* would be overlooked, from the three different CDs of music from or "inspired by" the film, to the incredible list of consultants that ran in the end credits and included such people as the Reverend Jesse Jackson; Christian right leader Pat Robertson; Rabbi Ismar Schorsch, head of the Jewish Theological Seminary of the Conservative movement; Rabbi Eric Yoffie, head of the Reform movement; Abraham Foxman of the Anti-Defamation League; Ralph Reed, late of the Christian Coalition; William Donahue of the Catholic League; Rabbi Norman Lamm, head of the Orthodox Yeshiva University; Moral Majority leader Jerry Falwell; Dr. Aziza Al-Hibri, a noted Islamic scholar; Salam Al-Marayati, one of the founders of the Muslim Public Affairs Council; and many, many others. It included Jews, Christians, and Muslims from a wide variety of viewpoints even within their respective faiths. For the most part DreamWorks publicity bragged about the literally hundreds of consultants who vetted the film, but it was short on details as to what that actually meant. Katzenberg claimed dozens of changes were made, and gave one example to a Christian weekly: a song lyric that was recorded as "You can work miracles when you believe" was changed to "There can be miracles when you believe." Said Katzenberg, "All three religious groups let us know that that line was a problem."

Even the phrasing of the title was calculated. According to the Bible, Moses escaped the fate of other Israelite male babies when he was sent on the river in a waterproof basket and discovered by Pharaoh's daughter. He was raised in the royal household, but his role in leading the Israelites to redemption and the Holy Land made him a pivotal figure in religious history. For Jews he was the Israelites' first prophet and their greatest teacher. For DreamWorks—founded by three Jews—he was an Egyptian prince. It wasn't so much that the Jewish component was denied (in the movie the Israelites even sing the biblical passage known as the "Song of the Sea" in Hebrew). It was the concern that if the movie appeared too Jewish-oriented it might alienate other moviegoers. Henry Herz, of the U.S. Catholic Conference, was asked by Katzenberg if the smiting of the Egyptian soldiers might be interpreted as a knock against present-day Islam. Here was the problem in a nutshell: the film tried so hard to round off corners and not upset anyone in any way whatsoever that it ended up being rather bland. As *Variety* put it, this was "a film that will be more admired than enjoyed."

Katzenberg had also boxed himself in on merchandising. Toys, games, plush dolls, fast-food tie-ins, and other ephemera had become part and parcel of the marketing of animated features geared to kids and their families. (This may have hit a low point in 1996, when Disney released an animated *Hunchback of Notre Dame* and one of the tie-in products was a backpack.) With *Prince of Egypt* Katzenberg was in a quandary. Was there a market for Golden Calf plush dolls or "Ten Plagues" Happy Meals? And even if there were people who would buy such kitsch, how would it reflect on the movie? Eventually the film would be released with minimal merchandising, mostly the CDs and some books.

At Katzenberg's insistence, *Prince of Egypt* was to avoid cuteness and easy comedy. It was his show, and the production team gave him what he wanted. Said Katzenberg, "We tried to be uncompromising here—there's nothing cute and adorable in the film. In other words, we didn't make the camel funny. You know how easy it is to make a camel funny?"

As the release date approached, nerves were fraying, and nothing was considered too minor to ignore. Pixar chairman and CEO Steve Jobs claimed that Katzenberg tried to bribe his company to push back the release of *A Bug's Life*. Jobs told *Newsweek*, "Jeffrey called us and asked us to convince Disney to delay the release of 'A Bug's Life' beyond the holiday 1998 season because that's when he wanted to release 'Prince of Egypt.' He said if we did that, he would kill 'Antz.' And we said, 'Don't go there.'" Katzenberg denied that he had made any such call.

Mike Ventrella, founder and editor of a small special-interest magazine called *Animato*, was quoted in *Entertainment Weekly* saying that for *Prince of Egypt* to live up to all its advance hype it would have to be a cross between the Second Coming and *Gone with the Wind*. Much to his surprise, he received a tart note from Terry Press, making it clear that the publicist thought someone like Ventrella had no right to criticize Katzenberg.

Publicly the DreamWorks line was that *Prince* was one of the prestige releases of the holiday movie season, and that it had been deliberately shifted from a Thanksgiving opening—avoiding conflict with *A Bug's Life*—to mid-December. Distribution chief Jim Tharp explained, "It's an event movie more than anything else. . . . The picture isn't strictly for kids; it's very adult, and with an obvious religious theme we felt it would maximize commercial potential by opening it during the prime filmgoing period at the end of the year, like *Titanic*."

When the film opened in December 1998 it was to solid if not rave reviews. It finally earned approximately $100 million at the box office in North America and another $100 million or so around the world. This made it the most successful non-Disney animation feature ever, eclipsing *Antz* in the process. Yet the $350 million that computer-animated *A Bug's Life* made in contrast to *Prince's* $200 million might have suggested that *Antz*—even though it made far less than either—would be a much more important indicator of DreamWorks's future than the hand-drawn *Prince of Egypt*.

The folks at DreamWorks were eagerly anticipating awards season. *Saving Private Ryan* had topped the box office and was winning critical kudos. It made more than 160 top-ten lists of the nation's critics, accumulating numerous awards from various critics groups and professional associations.

It won best picture and best director at the Golden Globes, an award that the public pays much more attention to than does Hollywood. Given by the Hollywood Foreign Press Association, the Golden Globes are largely a joke to Hollywood, taken seriously only because they are part of the campaign for the one award Hollywood cares about: the Oscar.

When the Oscar nominations were announced in February 1999, *Saving Private Ryan* was a major contender with eleven nominations, including Best Picture, Best Director, Best Actor (for Tom Hanks), and Best Original Screenplay (for Robert Rodat). There was just one problem: a late-December release, *Shakespeare in Love*, was up for thirteen awards. In spite of the fact that comedies rarely win the Oscar for Best Picture, suddenly *Saving Private Ryan* had serious competition. What made it especially ironic was that *Shakespeare in Love* was a Miramax film, and Miramax was owned by Disney. While neither Michael Eisner nor Jeffrey Katzenberg had much to do with the respective films, the battle between *Shakespeare* and *Ryan* seemed to be Oscar's proxy version of what had turned into the hottest lawsuit in Hollywood.

Miramax had been founded in 1979 by brothers Bob and Harvey Weinstein and named for their parents, Miriam and Max. Over the course of the 1980s, as they focused on art and independent films, the Weinsteins gained a reputation for having a magic touch. Their flops were buried and forgotten, but what people remembered were releases like *Pelle the Conqueror*; *The Thin Blue Line*; *sex, lies, and videotape*; *My Left Foot*; *Reservoir Dogs*; *The Crying Game*; and many others. Miramax brought new talent to light, found the best of the films doing the festival circuit, and, in the process, developed a reputation for being able to open hard-to-handle films successfully. In 1993 it was acquired by Disney, which gave the Weinsteins a guaranteed budget and a major corporation to back them, even if they occasionally had to bow to their new owners and revert to independent status for controversial films like *Kids* and *Fahrenheit 9/11*.

Miramax became an even bigger force under the Disney umbrella, handling such films as *Pulp Fiction*, *Sling Blade*, and *Good Will Hunting*. At Oscar time Miramax did not like to go home empty-handed, and it campaigned hard, even as it paid lip service to the industry pretense that it was not campaigning at all. *Shakespeare in Love* was its horse for 1998, and it opened to strong reviews and equally strong box office. Although it was a romantic comedy set in sixteenth-century England, it boasted a cast headed by Gwyneth Paltrow and turned out to be the surprise hit of the holiday movie season. *Saving Private Ryan* no longer had a lock on the Oscars. Indeed, *Ryan* had to contend with two Miramax releases up for Best Picture, the other being *Life Is Beautiful*, the daring Italian comedy set against the Holocaust, directed by and starring Roberto Benigni.

DreamWorks might have been playing in the big leagues now, but it had no idea what it was up against. As Peter Biskind recounted in his book about Miramax and the independent film scene, the Weinsteins were reported to have spent something on the order of $5 million for their Oscar campaign for *Shakespeare in Love*, whereas the average spent by a studio was less than half that. A magazine article claimed Bob Weinstein was bad-mouthing *Saving Private Ryan* in private conversation, a charge he denied. Indeed, he believed he himself was the victim of bad-mouthing and suggested that DreamWorks publicity chief Terry Press might be planting such rumors.

In fact some surprising articles slammed *Saving Private Ryan* in the run-up to the voting. *Variety*'s Peter Bart noted "the sudden outpouring of revisionist reviews of *Saving Private Ryan*." Author and screenwriter William Goldman denounced the film in *Premiere* magazine as "phony, manipulative shit" while veteran *New York Times* film critic Vincent Canby shared with readers his second thoughts that "a more or less commonplace WWII battle movie" had been overly praised.

In the end, *Saving Private Ryan* won five Oscars, including Best Director for Spielberg, but the other big prizes went to Miramax. DreamWorks couldn't really complain about Gwyneth Paltrow and Judi Dench getting the Best Actress and Best Supporting Actress awards, as *Ryan* had no female roles worth noting, but Tom Hanks lost to Roberto Benigni for Best Actor, and Best Picture and Best Original Screenplay went to *Shakespeare in Love*, which won seven awards. The DreamWorks crew was stunned. This was supposed to be the payoff for their blockbuster film, and while Spielberg won his second directing Oscar, they felt the big prize had been snatched away. After the ceremonies Terry Press sought out Harvey Weinstein to congratulate him, but according to one report she said to Katzenberg, "Never again!"

The next time DreamWorks faced off against Miramax, it would be prepared. As it turned out, it wouldn't have long to wait.

7

Open Wide

BESIDES THE LOSS of the Best Picture Oscar for *Saving Private Ryan*, 1999 was not shaping up as a good year for DreamWorks. Beyond the disappointment of the Academy Awards were fresh disappointments at the box office. *In Dreams*, Neil Jordan's surreal thriller with Aidan Quinn and Annette Bening, flopped, and *Forces of Nature*, a romantic comedy with hot stars Sandra Bullock and Ben Affleck, barely broke $50 million in domestic box office. *The Love Letter*, starring Kate Capshaw (Spielberg's wife), was a disaster financially, earning less than $10 million at box office. A big summer supernatural flick, *The Haunting* with Liam Neeson, at least made money, nearly cracking the $100 million mark domestically and topping $170 million in total grosses worldwide. About the only good news the troika received had nothing to do with DreamWorks: the judge in Katzenberg's lawsuit against Disney ruled for him. Disney would fight, even trying to subpoena DreamWorks financial documents as a way of getting Katzenberg to back off, but in the end Disney lost and paid up. (The amount was not disclosed, but it was estimated at $150 million.) While that was a relief, there wasn't much time to savor it. In July 1999 the Playa Vista studio deal finally collapsed.

In August DreamWorks continued its transition to a more traditional company where people had specifically defined roles. Katzenberg was named head of production for the studio, working with Walter Parkes and Laurie MacDonald on their upcoming films. Oddly, though, in his new role Katzenberg would answer to Parkes and MacDonald rather than the other way around. "I am an employee," he said. "I work for them." Industry mavens scratched their heads, but it made perfect sense to Katzenberg: "Between no litigation and no Playa Vista, my desk is empty. Animation is in unbelievably great shape right now. I have nothing to do, so they figured they'd put me to work."

"I know we don't fit people's preconceived notions of what a studio is, and we think that's a good thing," said Terry Press. Added MacDonald, "We don't want to disappoint those who've seen us as an eccentric company from the beginning. We want to stick to our tradition."

The real issue was that neither Spielberg nor Parkes and MacDonald wished to devote all their time to administrative duties overseeing other people's films. Spielberg was keeping his Amblin' Entertainment production company open for business, and DreamWorks had released only six films in 1998. The major studios ordinarily released three to four times that number. Indeed, with most of the majors now hosting several labels, that would seem to be the minimum. Suddenly letting Katzenberg—who *wanted* to be a movie studio boss—have more of a role made a lot of sense. "We've been fairly vocal in saying that there's only a certain extent to which we can change our stripes and become pure executives," Parkes told one interviewer. "We're happier focusing on a smaller number of pictures." When Spielberg declined to be interviewed, David Geffen emerged and assured everyone there was no talk of selling the studio or merging with Universal, Columbia, or anyone else.

There was nothing ailing DreamWorks that a lot more movies—and a few blockbuster hits—couldn't cure.

In September the debut film by stage director Sam Mendes began turning up at film festivals in Toronto and Boston, followed by limited releases in New York and Los Angeles. Slowly, as it was rolled out to theaters across the country, a quirky, dark, satiric film about a man having a midlife crisis and lusting after his teenage daughter's girlfriend was becoming the hot movie of the year. It was called *American Beauty*, and this time DreamWorks began rewriting the rules on how a studio should promote a film to the critics, the public, and, ultimately, the Oscar voters.

The idea for the movie had begun in the mind of writer Alan Ball, a struggling playwright then working in the art department of a New York–based magazine. As he would recount it, Ball was inspired by seeing a lurid comic-book version of the Joey Buttafuoco / Amy Fisher story—where a man was prepared to leave and perhaps kill his wife in order to be with his teenage lover. Wrote Ball, "What had become fodder for jokes on late-night talk shows was to those who had lived it genuine tragedy—and, no doubt, a far more complicated and interesting story than any we would ever hear. That realization—and an encounter with a plastic bag blowing in the wind outside the World Trade Center—was the basis for what would eventually become *American Beauty*." Ball started writing it as a stage play but put it aside for a few years. When he was ready to start writing again, he decided to develop it into a screenplay.

The screenplay was brought to the attention of Bob Cooper, then ostensibly heading up film production at DreamWorks, and he knew what to do: call Spielberg for permission to acquire it. He got the go-ahead and purchased it for $250,000, a tidy sum for Ball's first screenplay. When DreamWorks wanted to be daring they could be, as *American Beauty* went on to prove with the hiring of Mendes to direct. Already considered a *wunderkind* of the London and New York stages (with noted revivals of *Cabaret* and *Company* to his credit), Mendes edged out more experienced directors like Mike Nichols and Robert Zemeckis to bring *American Beauty* to the screen. Spielberg later told an interviewer, "I had seen his production of *Oliver!* on the London stage when I was making *Saving Private Ryan.* . . . I sort of banked his name in my mind."

Choosing Mendes proved to be a gamble. By his own account, the first three days of shooting were a disaster. "It was badly shot, my fault, badly composed, my fault, bad costumes, my fault," he later recalled. "And everybody was doing what I was asking. It was all my fault." Mendes got permission to scrap the footage and start again. Some very nervous DreamWorks executives approved, and the newly grounded director began again, having a new understanding of how the process worked.

Three years later, when Mendes was releasing his second DreamWorks film, *Road to Perdition*, Spielberg remembered it differently. According to Spielberg, who professed to be a Mendes booster, "[T]he first few days of *American Beauty* were very scary. I was looking at his footage, and I knew it wasn't going to cut together. I asked him to come over to my house, and we reviewed the footage together. In the end, he reshot the first three days, and from then on, he was perfect." This was the Spielberg touch at

DreamWorks: dropping in on a film, giving the key advice, and—if it turned out to be a success—quietly noting his own contribution.

Although *American Beauty* is really an ensemble piece, the focus of the story is Lester Burnham (Kevin Spacey) and his family. Lester is tired of his marriage, his job, his life. In the course of the film he quits his job, develops a rich fantasy life about a teenage girl (Mena Suvari) who goes to school with his daughter, smokes pot, and starts working out, all in an effort to climb out of the rut that is his life. Meanwhile his wife Carolyn (Annette Bening), an ambitious realtor, becomes involved professionally and personally with the local real estate kingpin (Peter Gallagher). The Burnhams' daughter Jane (Thora Birch) befriends Ricky (Wes Bentley), the strange son of their even stranger neighbors (Alison Janney, Chris Cooper). Ricky is recording his life on video, leading to the eerily poetic scene where he captures a plastic bag dancing in the wind with his camera.

If *Saving Private Ryan* had caught the new interest in the Greatest Generation, *American Beauty* perfectly captured American cynicism at the end of the twentieth century. The year before, President Bill Clinton had fought impeachment for what was essentially a tawdry affair with an intern. He was acquitted by the United States Senate and would leave office more popular than ever. Although not especially political, *American Beauty*'s Lester probably would have cheered on Clinton as someone who refused to conform to society's expectations even for the highest stakes. Ultimately Lester pulls back from his creepy obsession with his daughter's friend and finds the peace he's been seeking throughout the story.

American Beauty was a special film: it won over the critics, but it needed word of mouth to persuade audiences to take a chance on it, and it was an even longer haul for an Oscar campaign. Observers saw *American Beauty* repeating a pattern set by *L.A. Confidential*, which had opened to good reviews in 1997 and won the Oscar for Best Adapted Screenplay and Best Supporting Actress (for Kim Basinger) in a year when both awards and box office were swept up in the tidal wave for *Titanic*. Noted one entertainment industry reporter about *American Beauty*, "It's a mainstream-but-serious pic that critics have embraced as a signal that summer's over and thoughtful films have arrived." Other studios took note that *American Beauty* was first out of the box in the season's Oscar race and looked to counteract its momentum.

The film opened on September 15 on all of sixteen screens—what is known as a platform release. It would ride on the publicity and strong reviews from film festival showings and the New York and Los Angeles openings, then slowly expand as demand built for the film. Of course, there was a danger, as with *Amistad*, that the demand might not materialize. It was a calculated risk that made sense; a wide release would have meant a roll of the dice on one weekend for an odd film with no huge stars. The gamble paid off. The per-screen average on opening weekend was $54,000. The movie was hot in New York and Los Angeles. Would it play elsewhere?

The next weekend the film opened around the country in limited release on 429 screens. (A wide release—say *Spider-Man* or *Star Wars*—might easily play on 2,000 or 3,000 screens.) Platform releases are not unusual. What was unusual for *American Beauty* was that it was supposed to widen only to 100 screens on the second weekend and instead went to four times that number. Jim Tharp, DreamWorks's executive in charge of film distribution, threw out the game plan: "We had a very specific release plan for the film that we decided to change once it opened. Because it was so strong in those exclusive situations, we were able to get more screens and are literally making decisions about what to do on a week-by-week basis."

By early November *American Beauty* was on 1,000 screens, and its box office had increased by 59 percent. By contrast, the arty *The English Patient* had increased only 7 percent when it went wide in 1996, and even *Shakespeare in Love* went up only 26 percent. (*L.A Confidential* came closest in 1997 with a 46 percent boost upon increasing its screens.) DreamWorks masterfully played out the film's box office run, pulling it from most screens in December and January and then relaunching the movie on the strength of its Oscar nominations. In February it went from being on only eight screens in New York and Los Angeles to playing on 1,287 screens the next week—its *twenty-third* week in release. The movie had already grossed $75 million and would attract new audiences from its nominations and subsequent wins.

This time DreamWorks and Terry Press were leaving nothing to chance for the Oscars. Once again they were facing off against Miramax, which had released *The Cider House Rules* in December. Based on a best-selling novel by John Irving and directed by Miramax favorite Lasse Hallström, it featured a strong cast including Tobey Maguire, Charlize Theron, and Michael Caine. Hollywood was expecting a grudge match between the two studios after the preceding year's upset. Press made it clear she didn't want to spend a lot of money promoting her film for the Oscars, but she might not have any choice. "[W]inning awards ups the ante. If it gets Golden Globes, for example, then the spending levels increase," she explained. She painted herself as the victim of Miramax's aggressiveness. "It was Miramax that spent a lot of money first, and we did it in response. We did not initially plan to spend on the level that we did with *Saving Private Ryan*."

This time DreamWorks had the upper hand. *Cider House* had received mixed reviews and did disappointing business. Oscar handicappers began watching the various critics groups and guild awards. The Golden Globes named *American Beauty* best picture and also awarded it best director and screenplay. The Screen Actors Guild named Kevin Spacey best actor and Annette Bening best actress, though Chris Cooper lost to *Cider House*'s Caine. The Directors' Guild hailed Sam Mendes as best director, and he noted that he had not even been a member a year before.

In the audience the night of the Directors' Guild awards was Steven Spielberg, who was receiving the Guild's lifetime achievement award. It had long carried the name of D. W. Griffith, the first great American director, whose credits in the silent era included *Intolerance*, *Way Down East*, and *Broken Blossoms*. Unfortunately they also included *Birth of a Nation*, a 1915 masterpiece which was a landmark in film history but, alas, it also glorified the Ku Klux Klan. For a movie more than eighty years old, it remained the subject of controversy and heated debate, and so the Directors' Guild decided to remove Griffith's name from the award. Spielberg, revealing the shallowness of his supposed reverence for Hollywood history, told the audience, "You could have called it the Alan Smithee Award and I would be so proud to accept it." Alan Smithee is the fictional name put on a film when the actual director demands—usually over artistic differences—that his own name be removed.

When the Oscar nominations were announced, *Cider House Rules* picked up seven nominations, including Best

Picture, Best Director, Best Adapted Screenplay, and Best Supporting Actor (for Michael Caine), while *American Beauty* received eight, including Best Picture, Best Director, Best Actor, Best Actress, and Best Original Screenplay. This time there were no revisionist reviews deciding that *American Beauty* wasn't so wonderful after all. Indeed, it was still going strong as the Oscar show neared, topping $100 million in overseas box office, one of only three 1999 releases to have done so. (The other two were *Three Kings* and *Toy Story 2*.)

This time the big disappointment on Oscar night would be Annette Bening's, who had given what many considered the finest performance of her career in *American Beauty*. She lost to Hilary Swank for an equally impressive performance in *Boys Don't Cry*. *American Beauty* won a second Oscar for Kevin Spacey (who had previously won Best Supporting Actor for *The Usual Suspects*), and for director Sam Mendes, writer Alan Ball, and cinematographer Conrad Hall. *Cider House* won only two awards, neither in a category that included *American Beauty*: Best Supporting Actor for Michael Caine and Best Adapted Screenplay for John Irving, who had written the script from his own novel. Best of all, *American Beauty* took the top prize of the evening.

It was a triumph for DreamWorks as well as all concerned with the film, and the win had financial consequences. Those five Oscars helped the movie—now more than six months after its initial release—scoop up another $30 million. DreamWorks expanded *American Beauty* to two thousand screens, the most it had appeared on at any one time in two hundred days in release. Said *Variety*, "Most [studio distribution] vets agree that studio distrib chief Jim Tharp's game plan should serve as a textbook case." Indeed, the film would go on to a total of $130 million in domestic box office without ever being the number one film in the country on any given weekend. Total worldwide take was nearly $350 million.

Now if only DreamWorks could triple its output of films released each year, it might actually have a movie studio.

The DreamWorks 1999 awards blitz included a curious coda. In December, with little advance fanfare, the studio released a science-fiction comedy called *Galaxy Quest*, starring Tim Allen, Sigourney Weaver, and Alan Rickman. It was about the stars of a canceled television show similar to *Star Trek*, and the actors who now had little to show for their careers except appearing before adoring fans at conventions. It was done with imagination and affection as it told the story of how the actors must live up to their fictional roles when real aliens show up. The fans end up having to help the actors in order to save the day. It was a minor holiday season hit, eventually returning $90 million in worldwide grosses.

By Labor Day Weekend 2000, the folks at DreamWorks had other things on their minds than a modest genre comedy. Yet that weekend in Chicago real science-fiction fans (along with professional writers and artists) met from around the world for the fifty-eighth World Science Fiction Convention and the awarding of the field's top honor, the Hugos. The best dramatic presentation category included *The Iron Giant*, *The Sixth Sense*, *Being John Malkovich*, and the blockbuster that everyone assumed had the award locked up, *The Matrix*. Yet when the envelope was opened, *Galaxy Quest* won the prize. To the amazement of the assembled fans—who were used to being snubbed by Hollywood with someone at the convention having to accept the award on behalf of the winner—out strode director Dean Parisot and co-writer Robert Gordon to accept the Hugo Award in person.

DreamWorks didn't have to spend a dime to campaign for the award. Indeed, the assembled fans would have resented them if they had. Instead the studio simply picked up the tab for Parisot and Gordon to attend the convention, which turned out to be a gesture that was more appreciated by the fans than anything else the studio could have done.

8

In the Arena

WITH ITS Oscar triumph, DreamWorks had finally arrived as a movie studio. The talk was no longer of it being only a dream, but of a dream fulfilled. For roughly two years DreamWorks was at its peak. It may not have built a new studio at Playa Vista, but it did have the animator's "campus" in Glendale. Its music and TV divisions might be muddling along, but *American Beauty* was different. *Saving Private Ryan*, after all, owed more to Spielberg than to DreamWorks; the project had been in development at Paramount. *American Beauty*, on the other hand, was a film for which the DreamWorks principals were entitled to take the bows.

More success lay ahead, and even DreamWorks's failures would prove instructive to the industry. Unfortunately, at the time, failure began just five days after the Oscars with the release of DreamWorks's third animated film, *The Road to El Dorado*. On this project Katzenberg applied the Disney model to perfection. And as with *Antz* vs. *A Bug's Life*, there was a battle to get *El Dorado* into the theaters first.

"When we were doing *El Dorado*, Disney had a thing in the works, *The Emperor's New Groove*. It was really a race, and Katzenberg wanted ours out before theirs," recalled animator Marc Lumer, who worked on the visual development of the DreamWorks film. "We didn't know exactly what they were doing, but we had the impression it was going to be very similar. Whoever came out second would face the perception that they copied the other."

El Dorado used mostly traditional animation in telling the story of two adventurers searching for a city of gold in the New World. The voice cast included Kenneth Branagh, Kevin Kline, Rosie Perez, Armand Assante, and Edward James Olmos. The score was by Hans Zimmer, with songs by Elton John and Tim Rice, the very team behind the music for Disney's animated blockbuster *The Lion King*. If you looked at the ads, though, none of this was exploited, just as Disney did not sell its animated movies based on the talent. Instead—learning a lesson from the failure of *Prince of Egypt* to be the event they had hoped it would be—DreamWorks aggressively sought out partners to promote *El Dorado*.

"Because this was a broader-appeal movie than some we'd had before, we were freer to make these kinds of alliances," explained Brad Globe, who was head of DreamWorks Consumer Products. DreamWorks had promotional deals totaling $50 million in shared costs with Burger King, Hershey's, General Mills, Ralph's (a chain of groceries), and Loews Cineplex. Burger King was eager to try again, despite having been burned on their last team-up with the studio for the movie *Small Soldiers*. They had had all kinds of toys for their kids' meals when the somewhat violent film got slapped with a PG-13 rating. This time Burger King committed to distributing eight different *El Dorado* action figures over a four-week period, with displays in its fast-food restaurants plus a TV campaign promoting the tie-in. General Mills would have an "*El Dorado* Search for the

Gold Bar" on its Golden Grahams cereal, promoting the movie and offering a prize of a resort vacation.

The problem was that *El Dorado* was designed to appeal to an audience that had little interest in cartoons. Attracting youngsters and their families had not been a problem, and movies like *Aladdin* and *The Lion King* showed that adults would come out for an animated film given the right hook; but pre-teens and teens, particularly boys, had lost interest. *El Dorado* would be the first of several animated films to emphasize adventure over comedy. PG-rated animated action replaced the cute talking animals and slapstick. Japanese animation, or anime, had proved popular with some in this audience segment, so why couldn't Hollywood do it and do it better?

The Road to El Dorado opened on more than three thousand screens and took in less than $13 million on opening weekend. The movie was estimated to have cost $95 million; it earned only $50 million domestically and another $15 worldwide—a huge disappointment, and one that the competition—particularly Disney—seems to have learned nothing from observing. From initial conception to release, the animation process can take two to three years or more for a given film, and the films that would flop for Disney were already works in progress. *Atlantis: The Lost Empire* fizzled in the summer of 2001 (to DreamWorks's advantage) while *Treasure Planet*, a space-age retelling of *Treasure Island*, was pronounced dead on arrival when it appeared late in 2002. Likewise Don Bluth, who had scored a hit for Spielberg's Amblin' Entertainment with the 1986 *An American Tail* and who once was considered a potential rival for Disney, flopped a couple of months after *El Dorado* with the science-fiction saga *Titan A.E.*, done for Twentieth Century Fox.

DreamWorks would have its first big animated film hit that summer, but by that time it would just be a bonus.

There was much good news to make up for the disappointment of *El Dorado*. Woody Allen had had a public breakup with his producer, Jean Doumanian, in March 2000, and the following month it was announced that DreamWorks would now distribute his films. They were already handling his upcoming *Small Time Crooks*, and this would extend that deal by three films. In 2000 it was still possible to believe that Allen's recent slump was temporary, and that the creator of *Annie Hall, Manhattan, Hannah and Her Sisters*, and *Crimes and Misdemeanors* still had great films left in him. Used to his independence, with a deal that allowed him total control of his films, Allen had actually freelanced on some Katzenberg projects. He had done one of the segments of the Disney triptych *New York Stories* and had appeared with Bette Midler in Paul Mazursky's disappointing *Scenes from a Mall*. More recently he had been the starring voice in DreamWorks's own *Antz*.

Then Sam Mendes, the first-time movie director and Oscar winner for *American Beauty*, renewed his ties with DreamWorks with a two-year "first look" deal. DreamWorks didn't have to do his films, but they would have first crack at them. Mendes received $500,000 up front and also got DreamWorks to cough up $160,000 per year to his theater group for its low-budget productions.

On May 2 the summer season kicked off early with *Gladiator*. Getting a jump over the traditional start of the summer movie season on Memorial Day weekend, DreamWorks hoped an early release would encourage lightning to strike. It did—repeatedly. Audiences had been primed for *Gladia-*

tor as early as the previous winter's Super Bowl, where DreamWorks paid top dollar to run a spot for a movie that wouldn't be out for months.

Walter Parkes had been working with producer Doug Wick to develop the project, and pitched it to director Ridley Scott with two things in hand: a second draft of the screenplay by David Franzoni and a reproduction of the French painting *Pollice Verso* by Jean-Léon Gérôme, wherein a gladiator awaits the emperor's decision of thumbs up or thumbs down for his vanquished opponent. According to Parkes after he made his pitch, Scott was mesmerized by the painting. Finally Scott pointed to it and said, "I can do that." The movie is the story of General Maximus (Russell Crowe) who, in gaining the trust of Emperor Marcus Aurelius (Richard Harris), makes a bitter enemy of the emperor's son Commodus (Joaquin Phoenix). Commodus murders his father and arranges for the slaughter of Maximus's wife and child. Maximus ends up in slavery and then as a gladiator. He becomes more popular than ever, to the shock of Commodus who thought him dead. This leads to a preposterous battle to the death between Maximus and Commodus, and an ahistorical return to the Roman republic.

Audiences didn't care if they had to suspend their disbelief. This was the first swords-and-sandals epic since the 1960s. For most moviegoers, such films as *Quo Vadis* (1951), *Ben-Hur* (1959), and *Spartacus* (1960) were movies they had seen on television, if at all. Like such entries as the Western *Dances with Wolves* and the musical *Chicago*, *Gladiator* came at a time when the genre it was part of was moribund and largely forgotten. This gave director Ridley Scott the freedom to reinvent it, and it made even the hoariest clichés seem fresh and original to younger moviegoers, who had no familiarity with these types of films. *Gladiator* became a phenomenal success. With virtually no competition, it took in $35 million opening weekend and went on to earn more than $187 million just in domestic box office. Add nearly $270 million in foreign box office, and it was clear that this was DreamWorks's second-biggest hit after *Saving Private Ryan*.

But the studio was just warming up. A few weeks later the moronic *Road Trip* opened. It made no apologies. With a cast that included Tom Green and Seann William Scott, it was *supposed* to be moronic. The humor was rude and crude, with sex and drug references meant to appeal to teens (at least those who could evade the R rating) and twenty-somethings. The low-cost film nearly covered its budget of $15.6 million on its opening weekend, and raked in more than $100 million worldwide. It wasn't a blockbuster, but it wasn't meant to be. It was a gross-out comedy geared to younger viewers, and was easily in profits before launching its ancillary cable and video windows. At the opposite extreme was *Small Time Crooks*, the first Woody Allen comedy to be released through DreamWorks. It was decidedly minor Allen and, in retrospect, would be seen as part of his long decline over the ensuing decade; but the film covered its modest production costs in U.S. release and eventually turned a profit from foreign markets and home video sales.

In late June DreamWorks released its second animated feature for the year. This one wasn't developed in house but was done by Aardman Animation, a British company well known for its short *Wallace and Gromit* films about a cheese-loving Englishman and his dog. *Chicken Run* was a hilarious send-up of prisoner-of-war films, in which a group of chickens plan their escape from a farm that is converting its output from eggs to chicken potpies. Rocky, the ringleader of the escape, is a newly arrived chicken who is known to fly as part of his circus act. Rocky is voiced by Mel Gibson, with a British cast, including Miranda Richardson and Timothy Spall, in other roles. Aardman's house style was neither traditional cel animation nor computer animation, but stop-motion photography involving clay models. It was painstaking work, but it was their own.

As with *El Dorado*, DreamWorks developed marketing partners, and this time it worked. Burger King promoted the film with a campaign that said, "Save the chickens. Eat a Whopper." British Airways had a "Fly the Coop to London" promotion. The studio also arranged promotions on the children's cable channel Nickelodeon and the syndicated game show *Wheel of Fortune*. Deals were made with several other companies, including Chevron, Clorox, and Kroger supermarkets.

Now the hits just kept coming. *What Lies Beneath*, a thriller from director Robert Zemeckis, starring Michelle Pfeiffer and Harrison Ford, was the last of the studio's summer releases. It was a runaway smash, earning more than $155 million at the U.S. box office and another $120 million worldwide. Of DreamWorks's summer releases, *Gladiator*, *Chicken Run*, and *What Lies Beneath* all topped $100 million in the United States, and *Road Trip*, which had cost $15 million, did that worldwide. The Woody Allen film was a disappointment, but in the long run it didn't lose money. As if to show that its movie arm was what would make or break DreamWorks, stories now began appearing in the press about how well the company was doing, even though it had released only six films so far that year, had shut down or sold off its interactive projects, and wasn't able to get much traction in the television or music business. In Hollywood, movies are king, and in the summer of 2000 Russell Crowe's triumph in the arena in *Gladiator* was a metaphor for DreamWorks's startling run of success.

Production heads Walter Parkes and Laurie MacDonald had renewed their contracts in May, allowing them to produce their own films for the studio as well as shepherding others through production. Said Parkes, "As DreamWorks has matured, we're spending less time just building the company." The goal was to boost the production schedule to ten or eleven films a year, including one or two animated features. By midsummer, *Variety*'s annual look at the studio was the most upbeat it had been since the troika's initial press conference nearly six years earlier: "Hollywood is finally taking note: DreamWorks has truly arrived." In addition to its 2000 hits, *American Beauty* had continued to earn from its Oscar success and had finally come out on video. Even the failure of *El Dorado* was pushed aside since DreamWorks's first two animated releases, *Antz* and *Prince of Egypt*, held the records for highest non-Disney animated grosses. Twentieth Century Fox and Warner Bros. had had a run at Disney, Fox with *Anastasia* and *Titan A.E.*, Warners with *Quest for Camelot*, and both had fallen short. Under Katzenberg's supervision, DreamWorks's animated films were still very much in the game.

What had been clucked at as DreamWorks's quirkiness was now excused as part of its charm, since you can't argue with success. *Entertainment Weekly* practically swooned in its end-of-summer review: "DreamWorks is teaching Hollywood a lesson in smart marketing, leaving no demographic stone unturned." Even though the number one box office movie for the summer was Paramount's *Mission: Impossible II*, and even though Disney's overall slate (including the animated *Dinosaur* and the action film *Gone in 60 Seconds*) gave the studio its sixth summer at number one in total box office, DreamWorks was the story. That the upstart studio was number two behind Disney was what the industry noticed. Hollywood may not have understood what Dream-Works was doing, but it respected the results. Or as one observer put it, "It's a dysfunctional studio, but if you look at the product you've got to say it's a dysfunctional studio that works very well."

When DreamWorks pulled the plug on Pop.com over the Labor Day weekend, no one—except its employees and contractors—was paying attention. What people wanted to know was, how long could the studio keep its hit machine rolling? It fell short almost immediately with the fall release of *Almost Famous*, Cameron Crowe's semi-autobiographical film about a fifteen-year-old would-be rock journalist's adventures on the road following a band and its groupies. It was inspired by Crowe's real-life experiences following the Allman Brothers band on tour at a relatively early age. It received great reviews, and Kate Hudson, in her breakout film role, was singled out for special praise for her turn as the groupie Penny Lane. There was just one problem: audiences weren't interested in this exercise in baby-boomer nostalgia. It also demonstrated that Cameron Crowe had a loyal but quite limited audience.

Crowe had expanded from rock criticism to journalism and finally broke into the movies when he adapted his *Fast Times at Ridgemont High* into the 1982 film that made Sean Penn a star. As a writer/director Crowe wrote passionate, funny, and emotional films that connected with some people but left most viewers cold. *Say Anything* and *Singles* may have devoted followings, but neither burned up the box office. Crowe got lucky with his third film, *Jerry Maguire*. With Tom Cruise as star, a heartfelt turn by Renée Zellweger, and an Oscar-winning performance from Cuba Gooding, Jr., in his "Show me the money!" part, it was a smash hit. Such success lets a filmmaker write his own ticket—usually for one or two films anyway—and Crowe decided to do *Almost Famous*. Poor box office ensured that it soon vanished from sight, but it would be back.

The box office failure of *Almost Famous* mystified both director and studio. Crowe and DreamWorks executives reportedly blamed each other, but publicly they were mutually supportive while continuing to back the film. Crowe expressed gratitude that the studio had let him make it the way he wanted. Jeffrey Katzenberg remarked, "We are hurt and despondent that it has not done more at the box [office]—that's our shared disappointment. . . . I think we may have been the right movie at the wrong time."

It turned out that DreamWorks's success was as much by luck as by design. One 2000 release, an Australian production called *Walk the Talk*, was considered so bad it was buried after an appearance at the 2000 Toronto Film Festival, going directly to video in the United States. Rod Lurie's lurid and overwrought *The Contender*, with Joan Allen as a vice-presidential candidate facing smears about her past, was dead on arrival. Robert Redford's period golfing film, *The Legend of Bagger Vance*—boasting a cast that included Matt Damon, Will Smith, Charlize Theron, and, in his final film, Jack Lemmon—didn't score well either. Barry Levinson's odd comedy about Northern Ireland wig salesmen, *An Everlasting Piece*, barely even registered. (This wouldn't be the last time Barry Levinson, the maker of such films as *Rain Man* and *Avalon*, would direct a disastrous misfire for DreamWorks.)

DreamWorks did have two more hits in store, but both were co-productions in which the studio held only foreign rights. They were good for the company's bottom line but offered nothing in the way of publicity at home. *Meet the Parents* was partnered with Universal and *Castaway* with Twentieth Century Fox. It was a good way to share the burden of the films' budgets, but the downside included having to share profits. David Geffen, it was said, had developed a specialty in negotiating these deals. *Gladiator* had also been a co-production, with Universal, but because DreamWorks held U.S. distribution rights, the coming awards campaign would be its responsibility (and to its credit). DreamWorks decided it had a winner in *Gladiator*, and that's the film it pushed in the year's Oscars race.

In November *Gladiator* was released on DVD, offering a perfect opportunity for a big event that, not so incidentally, promoted the film to Oscar voters. The movie was screened at the Samuel Goldwyn Theater, followed by *Variety*'s chief critic Todd McCarthy interviewing director Ridley Scott.

When the various critics groups began to announce their awards, though, something funny happened. No one expected *Gladiator* to be a contender. In spite of good reviews, it wasn't that sort of film. Russell Crowe picked up kudos here and there, as did Joaquin Phoenix and some of the behind-the-scenes talent (such as cinematographer John Mathieson). Surprisingly, it was DreamWorks's fall flop, *Almost Famous*, that was racking up critical prizes. Awards for Kate Hudson and Frances McDormand (who played the protagonist's mother) might have been expected, perhaps, as were the awards for Crowe's screenplay. But when the Boston Society of Film Critics named *Almost Famous* best picture of the year on December 17 it created a bit of a stir. The Boston critics group is known for its sometimes eccentric choices. Not as old or as influential as such groups in New York or Los Angeles, it had pushed its award announcements to the same mid-December weekend when the more prestigious New York and Los Angeles announcements are made in order to increase the impact of the Boston choices.

Cameron Crowe later suggested that the move by the Boston critics put his film back on the map. In ensuing weeks *Almost Famous* picked up more citations, including best picture from critics groups in Chicago, Phoenix, and San Diego as well as the Online Film Critics Society and the Southeastern Film Critics Association. When it won a Golden Globe for best picture—since the Hollywood Foreign Press Association distinguishes between musical/comedy and drama, *Gladiator* also won—the Academy voters knew this was a film they had to see, having presumably missed its run in the theaters months before. Screenings were arranged and videos sent out. DreamWorks suddenly had another contender in the Oscar race.

When the Oscar nominations were announced, DreamWorks was not only a contender but a major player. *Gladiator* received the most nominations with twelve, including Best Picture, Best Actor, Best Supporting Actor, and Best Original Screenplay. Its closest competition was Ang Lee's martial-arts fantasy, *Crouching Tiger, Hidden Dragon*, with ten nominations. The Miramax powerhouse had a rough year, with its designated Oscar pick, *Chocolat*, the latest from *Cider House Rules* director Lasse Hallström, gaining only five nominations. *Traffic* and *Erin Brockovich* were also in the running. Even two fall flops from DreamWorks produced half a dozen nominations between them. *The Contender*'s Joan Allen and Jeff Bridges each won acting nods, and *Almost Famous* received nominations for Kate Hudson,

Frances McDormand, Crowe's screenplay, and film editing. It was a competitive field, with perhaps *Gladiator* and *Crouching Tiger* considered the favorites. The outcome was hard to predict, but it looked highly unlikely that Dream-Works would go home empty-handed on Oscar night.

At the end of the evening of March 25, 2001, Dream-Works movies had earned awards in six categories, including Best Picture for the second year in a row. *Gladiator* star Russell Crowe won for Best Actor (with some saying it was another example of an actor deserving the award but getting it for the wrong movie, as Crowe's middle-aged tobacco company executive in 1999's *The Insider* was deemed a better performance). The film also won for costumes, sound, and visual effects. It was the first time a movie had won for Best Picture and had lost both Best Director (which went to *Traffic*'s Steve Soderbergh) and Best Screenplay. The trio of writers credited with the original *Gladiator* script—David Franzoni, John Logan, and William Nicholson—were no doubt disappointed. Yet DreamWorks executives could smile when the envelope was opened: the winner was Cameron Crowe for *Almost Famous*. For a change, the critics had had an impact.

The Oscars marked the end of the 2000 movie season—even as the 2001 movie season was already nearly three months old—and DreamWorks was in its glory. It had enjoyed financial success, however tempered by partnerships with other studios, and had the tremendous satisfaction of winning Best Picture two years running. Was this the fruition of its plan? Did the people running DreamWorks know what they were doing, or had they just been incredibly lucky?

9

Easy Being Green

WHEN A STUDIO releases a string of hit films, everyone who works there is assumed to be a genius. The studio is said to have a magic touch. Such was DreamWorks in 2000, the failures conveniently forgotten. If a studio has a bad year but releases a film that's such a huge success it overshadows everything else, that can work too. Such was DreamWorks in 2001.

Most of the films released or co-produced by Dream-Works that year were eminently forgettable. A teaming of two of the hottest stars in the business, Brad Pitt and Julia Roberts, resulted in *The Mexican*, a lackluster effort in which, amazingly, the two shared little screen time together. It earned more than $100 million worldwide, but it was nothing extraordinary.

A.I.: Artificial Intelligence was one of Steven Spielberg's most misconceived efforts, an attempt to pick up a project first developed by the late Stanley Kubrick, about a childless family that adopts a little boy robot (cloyingly played by Haley Joel Osment) and his subsequent dark misadventures. Kubrick's and Spielberg's sensibilities were a total mismatch, and this intended summer blockbuster earned less than $80 million in the United States. In this case DreamWorks was fortunate in that Warner Bros. was saddled with the U.S. release while DreamWorks had most of the overseas theatrical rights, and the film earned nearly twice as much abroad.

Evolution, a science-fiction comedy from Ivan Reitman and starring David Duchovny, also disappointed. They were hoping for another *Ghostbusters*, but it went nowhere. The film made less than $40 million in the United States. Columbia, which co-produced, made less than $30 million in foreign sales.

At the end of the summer came the next Woody Allen film, and now the once great director's slide to irrelevancy could no longer be denied. *Curse of the Jade Scorpion* might have worked as a Bob Hope comedy in the 1940s, but in 2001 the idea of Woody Allen and Helen Hunt being hypnotized into performing crimes was simply lame. The film took in just $12 million worldwide, less than half its estimated $26 million budget.

Fortunately, none of this mattered. On May 18 DreamWorks's first computer-animated film since *Antz* was released. It was called *Shrek*.

Shrek was loosely based on a picture book by William Steig. It took little from Steig's distinctive artwork. Steig's ogre was funny but hideous looking. The donkey was a minor character who recited poetry, not wisecracks. And the unnamed princess the ogre marries was always hideous looking and not under any spells, sleeping or transformative. The book had been brought to Jeffrey Katzenberg's attention by Laurie MacDonald, and Katzenberg saw the potential for it and acquired the movie rights. It was Katzenberg who saw this as a computer animation showcase for DreamWorks's Pacific Data Images (PDI), the company it had acquired a stake in and eventually bought out. Katzenberg explained, "The story itself was sort of a fractured fairy tale, and I thought the animation technique should be as different as the story and the sensibility of the movie."

Comedian Chris Farley was signed to voice the green ogre, but his death in December 1997 nearly derailed a year's worth of work. In one of the ways that would come to distinguish DreamWorks from Disney animation, the film had been built around Farley's personality, which had been allowed to inhabit and define Shrek. With the exception of Robin Williams's genie in *Aladdin*, Disney's voice actors were secondary to the animated characters. *Shrek* got back on track with the signing of Mike Myers, who brought his own sensibility that would influence both the script and the look of the film.

Katzenberg had a moment of panic when Myers saw the film with his voice track. Myers hadn't found the voice for Shrek, later recalling it sounded like Myers himself with a thicker Canadian accent. Myers asked that they scrap his audio recording track and let him start again as he searched for the perfect voice for the character. Explained Katzenberg, "I don't think Mike understood what was going on in my mind, which was that literally one third of [the scenes with] his character had already been animated." Katzenberg could have been the budget-conscious boss and told Myers to live with it, but instead he let the actor have his way. That decision added an estimated $4 million to the film's budget, since now the animators would have to redo numerous scenes so that Shrek's lip movements would match Myers's new line readings. But when Myers came back with the new Shrek voice—which he described as "the

Scottish accent of somebody who's lived in Canada twenty years"—Katzenberg knew he had made the right choice. "It was like we had junk and now we had gold," he said.

One of the things very much on everyone's mind was that *Shrek* had a similar premise to *Beauty and the Beast*, with a monster and a beautiful maiden who end up in love. Both had also recast the traditional heroic characters—Gaston the hunter, Lord Farquaad—as bullying, cowardly villains. The similarities ended there. For all its invention and entertainment value as one of the greatest of Disney's animated features, *Beauty and the Beast* remains a traditional fairy tale, or at least a modern Disneyized version of one. *Shrek* would have a very different sensibility, starting with surrounding the ogre with storybook characters whom he treats with annoyance and contempt. Shrek would get his moment to win over the audience when we see how his blustery exterior hides his own insecurities, but he would remain a sarcastic, wisecracking ogre who relished his monsterhood.

The rest of the casting was similarly inspired. Eddie Murphy had played a tiny dragon in Disney's animated *Mulan* (1998), where he was trapped in the necessities of the plot. Here, as Donkey, he was allowed to improvise and free-associate his lines, making the character his own. Murphy had been the first choice for Donkey. Cameron Diaz, not previously known for animation voice work, played Princess Fiona, and she was cast just after she had completed *There's Something About Mary* but before the film had been released. John Lithgow, an actor known for both comedic and dramatic roles, was the evil Lord Farquaad. The ad campaign trumpeted this prestige cast rather than letting the audience discover it in newspaper feature stories or through reading the closing credits. Posters listed Myers,

Murphy, Diaz, and Lithgow as the *stars* of the film, even though only their voices would be heard. Here, as with any ordinary live-action film, the names of the principal cast members were treated as promotable elements, to good effect.

While everyone involved in DreamWorks was clearly trying to make the best and most entertaining film they could, they sensed that *Shrek* would be something different. If it wasn't quite the "anti-Disney" film, still there was the chance to make fun of Katzenberg's former employer in ways that audiences would find appealing. One such moment occurs when Shrek arrives at Lord Farquaad's castle and finds a huge rope line with a sign indicating how long a wait it will be from that point until he is finally admitted. Shrek goes barreling through the ropes instead. Anyone who had ever stood in line at a Disney theme park could immediately relate.

When *Shrek* was entered in competition at the prestigious Cannes Film Festival, it was the first time an animated feature had competed since 1974, when the countercultural *Nine Lives of Fritz the Cat* was invited. At the press conference at Cannes, the DreamWorks team didn't shy away from the obvious. Co-director Vicky Jensen admitted the studio was pushing the limits of the *Beauty and the Beast* story. Katzenberg observed, "*Shrek* has a very subversive attitude and tone throughout the movie. It is very much part of the tapestry and design of the film in every respect. We are quite playful with many aspects of culture, some of which are Disney, but there are many, many others also. . . . We take shots at everybody." Katzenberg insisted that everything was intended to be good-natured fun, but not everyone agreed. *Newsweek* noted, "In this version of things, Cinderella bitch-slaps Snow White, an adorable Gingerbread Man screams 'Eat me!' and when the heroine breaks into sweet song, her soprano is so shrill it causes birds to explode. It doesn't take a detective to sniff out the subtext here: DreamWorks is taking potshots at its animation rival, Disney." For his part, Katzenberg played down the notion of a vendetta and even sent a copy of *Shrek* to Disney to make sure there was nothing in it to give offense.

Although it won no prizes at Cannes, the reviews for *Shrek* were sensational. *Variety* called it "an instant animated classic." Lisa Schwarzbaum, in *Entertainment Weekly*, saw it as a pivotal film in DreamWorks's short history, "This charmingly loopy, iconoclastic story about a crotchety ogre, a rakish donkey, a princess with a beauty secret, and a contemptible nobleman with a Napoleon complex isn't only a funny, sprightly fable for all ages about not judging a book by its cover; it's also a kind of palace coup, a shout of defiance, and a coming-of-age for DreamWorks, the upstart studio that shepherded the project with such skill and chutzpah."

Once again, promotional tie-ins were key. *Shrek* was launched with $100 million in cross-promotional ventures with Baskin-Robbins, Burger King, Heinz, Chevron, and American Licorice. Heinz, which had introduced E-Z Squirt ketchup bottles the previous October, now offered bottles of red ketchup with Princess Fiona's image—and green ketchup with that of Shrek. Kroger supermarkets ran a promotion that offered two free tickets to *Shrek* to qualifying customers, running ads to promote the giveaway and, not so incidentally, promote the film.

When it was released, *Shrek* did gangbusters at the box office. It made $42 million opening weekend, which made it the biggest DreamWorks opening ever, better than *Gladiator*.

Here was the animated hit that Katzenberg had been hungering for, drawing in not only families but also adults without kids. Children responded to the fairy-tale aspects and slapstick, adults liked the cast and the topical references which, besides the Disney potshots, included takeoffs of *The Matrix*, *The Dating Game*, and other pop culture touchstones. The next weekend—the traditional Memorial Day kickoff to summer—the film's grosses went even higher, with a take of $55 million. Even sweeter for DreamWorks was that in June Disney released its summer animated offering, *Atlantis: The Lost Empire*. It's hard to say that any movie that earned $184 million worldwide was a disappointment, but *Atlantis* underperformed for a Disney film. (Only $84 million was from the U.S. box office.) By comparison, *Shrek* made nearly $270 million in domestic ticket sales and another $200 million worldwide. It wasn't even close. DreamWorks and Disney had gone head to head on a summer animated film, and the Disney film had earned less than half of *Shrek*'s take. There was immediately talk of a *Shrek* sequel.

Students of the DreamWorks/Disney rivalry realized there was something else to be considered. In 2001 the Academy Awards would for the first time include a new category for Best Animated Feature. There had been Oscars for animated shorts for decades, and Disney had won its fair share, but there had never been enough animated features to warrant a separate category. Indeed, Walt Disney had been given an honorary Oscar for *Snow White*, which included seven little Oscars to go with it. Now, in this new category, if the competition were to come down to *Shrek* vs. *Atlantis*, it wouldn't even be close. It would be impossible for DreamWorks not to take home the statuette in a category that might never have existed but for Disney.

"To be sure, DreamWorks still runs counter to conventional wisdom about show business. It controls no vast library, no theme parks, no global distribution mechanism. At a moment in time when everyone obsesses about the wafer-thin profits of the film business, DreamWorks essentially remains a pure film play."

Thus wrote *Variety* editor-in-chief—and former studio executive—Peter Bart, in the wake of the studio's Oscar wins and in anticipation of *Shrek*'s success, which he noted could turn into a major moneymaker for DreamWorks. While industry observers were still buzzing about the studio's success the previous summer and at the Oscars, Bart was looking behind the curtain and noticing that the studio still did not operate in anything approaching a normal fashion. Katzenberg, who was supposed to be the new production chief answering to Parkes and MacDonald, just as quickly seemed to have given up the job. His time was taken up with the animation division in general and with *Shrek* in particular.

Thus it was little surprise in June when Michael DeLuca emerged as the new production head at DreamWorks. DeLuca had been ousted from his executive perch at New Line Cinemas. He turned down a chance to be a producer with a three-year $105 million deal at New Line, choosing instead to move to DreamWorks. The studio was no longer playing the game of no titles for its executives. DeLuca was named president of film production, becoming the first executive there to have a title to go along with office and salary. He would report not only to Parkes and MacDonald but also to Katzenberg.

At summer's end DreamWorks was still riding high on *Shrek*—and ignoring its lackluster slate of live-action films.

In August the studio announced a December opening for *Shrek* in Japan, with both dubbed and subtitled prints. The dubbed version would feature the voices of big Japanese stars who could be promoted as Myers, Murphy, Diaz, and Lithgow had been. Movie and TV star Masatoshi Hamada would play Shrek while model Morika Fujiwara would be Fiona. Donkey would be voiced by television star Kouichi Yamadera. Movie and TV actor Masato Ibu would play Lord Farquaad. This recasting of voice actors in different countries would happen elsewhere as well; Disney had been doing it for years.

At summer's end *Shrek* was the biggest hit of the 2001 season, outperforming *The Mummy Returns* and *Pearl Harbor*, though *Mummy*'s worldwide figures edged out *Shrek*. It was not that *Shrek* didn't travel well; it would eventually earn more than $200 million in foreign ticket sales. It was simply that the film was opening more slowly overseas. (And it would nonetheless rank second worldwide at year's end, the number one slot going to box office phenomenon *Harry Potter and the Sorcerer's Stone*, the first of the screen adaptations of J. K. Rowling's immensely popular series of books.)

On September 11, when America was stunned by the terrorist attacks on the World Trade Center in New York and the Pentagon in Washington, Hollywood had to react along with everyone else. For the movie industry it had to do with pulling or erasing anything that might remind people of the horror. In the Ben Stiller comedy *Zoolander*, the image of the World Trade Center was digitally removed. The Arnold Schwarzenegger action film *Collateral Damage*, about a man going after the terrorists who had caused the death of his family, was pushed back to 2002. *Sidewalks of New York*, an innocuous romantic comedy, was held back in order to remove the Twin Towers from the film's advertising and even from establishing shots in the movie itself.

DreamWorks had *The Last Castle*, another Rod Lurie potboiler (though he had not written it as he had *The Contender*), this time with Robert Redford as a court-martialed general sent to a prison run by a martinet (James Gandolfini) and eventually helping to lead a revolt. The film had no direct connection to the news, but the idea of a movie in which at least some members of the American military were portrayed in a bad light "arrives at a tricky moment," according to one review. The film did virtually no business and quickly disappeared.

As the country was urged to return to normalcy lest "the terrorists win," the studios jockeyed for position. Disney's contender for the animated feature Oscar, the Pixar-produced *Monsters, Inc.*, was set for release on Friday, November 2—the same day *Shrek* was released on video. It was no coincidence. Videos are normally released on Tuesdays in the U.S. market, so this was a deliberate attempt by DreamWorks to do what Disney had done to its animation rivals: undercut the launch of the competition.

The *Shrek* DVD contained bonus extras, including an additional musical finale that had not appeared in theaters. In its first three days of release on videocassette and DVD, *Shrek* recorded an incredible $110 million in sales. Although still short of the record holder—Disney's *The Lion King*—the video release of *Shrek* had already surpassed the year's previous biggest seller, *Star Wars Episode I: The Phantom Menace*. The movie was priced to sell, and though rentals were high, Universal, which handled DreamWorks video releases, was deluged with orders for additional copies. Disney had no cause to complain, though. *Monsters, Inc.* had a $62 million opening weekend, setting a new record for animated features.

As the Oscar nomination process loomed once again, DreamWorks's lackluster live-action slate had nothing in contention for Best Picture after three nominations and two consecutive wins. While DreamWorks was a partner with Universal on *A Beautiful Mind*, Universal held domestic rights, so DreamWorks had no part of the Oscar campaign for that film.

Instead its focus was on the animation category where thirteen features vied for one of three slots. Disney's strongest candidate was *Monsters, Inc.*, but while Disney benefited greatly from its release of the film—and marketing it through its theme parks, publishing, dolls, etc.—it remained a Pixar production. Pixar had been enjoying great success at Disney, but tensions were growing between the two companies. (They came to a head after the release of *The Incredibles* in 2004, when Pixar announced it would be looking to make a new deal with a different studio after the release of *Cars*, the final film under their Disney contract. That changed in early 2006, after Michael Eisner left Disney, when the company agreed to be acquired by Disney.) If Pixar won the Oscar, would it really be to Disney's credit? For Oscar handicappers there was also the issue of whether the new category served to ghettoize animation. Some, including DreamWorks publicist Terry Press, felt that *Shrek* was the first animated feature since *Beauty and the Beast* to have a shot at the Best Picture nomination.

In addition to pushing *Shrek* for both Best Picture and Best Animated Feature, ads appeared in the trade papers pushing Eddie Murphy for Best Supporting Actor for his voice work as Donkey. "If the nominations go to the actor that gives the best performance, how can you not vote for what Eddie Murphy did in this film?" asked Press. In the end her campaign wouldn't pay off at the Oscars, but it did earn Murphy a nomination from the British Academy of Film & Television Arts (BAFTA).

Disney decided to back *Monsters, Inc.* as its best shot. Said one Disney executive, "We're putting everything behind *Monsters*. We're passionate about the genre. It's what this studio stands for." The "for your consideration" ads for *Shrek* in the trades pointedly did not focus on the animation category. Said Press, "It's obvious that it's an animated film. I'm sure people will presume that *Shrek* will show up in the animation category." Still, there was a lot of sentiment for Disney. As one industry reporter put it, "[I]f ever there was an award that seems to be Disney's corporate birthright, it's the best toon prize."

When the Oscar nominations were announced, *Monsters, Inc.* was nominated in three categories while *Shrek* was named in only two. They would go head to head for the Best Animated Feature (the third nominee, the low-budget and amusing *Jimmy Neutron: Boy Genius*, was just along for the ride). *Monsters, Inc.* was also nominated for Best Sound Editing and Best Song while *Shrek* was nominated for Best Adapted Screenplay.

It was a year with no clear winners in most of the races, and it turned into one of the ugliest Oscar campaigns ever. Stories began appearing that Ron Howard had deliberately omitted the fact that the mentally disturbed mathematician John Nash, the subject of his *A Beautiful Mind*, had written a letter years before containing anti-Semitic remarks. Since the film pulled no punches about the fact that Nash was seriously delusional, as Nash himself noted in responding to the smear campaign, the arrival of these stories during the Oscar voting was thought to be an underhanded way to influence the voters.

The high-pressure campaign for *Shrek* did not go into attack mode, but some felt it was still a bit much. Perhaps one of the most interesting and nuanced ads appeared in early March. Legendary Warner Bros. animator Chuck Jones, the man responsible for some of the greatest Bugs Bunny and Road Runner shorts among other items in a long career, had died. DreamWorks took out an ad that read simply "Chuck Jones 1912–2002" and featured a backlit and somber picture of Shrek with a bowed head. It was a touching tribute, but Jones had had nothing whatsoever to do with DreamWorks. The subtext of the message was as pointed as the surface message was respectful: Dream-Works, home of the most popular animated film of the last year, was paying homage to another giant of the animation field.

On Oscar night, *Shrek* lost the adapted screenplay award (which went to Akiva Goldman for the Universal/DreamWorks co-production of *A Beautiful Mind*, the evening's big winner). *Monsters, Inc.* lost the sound editing award, but Randy Newman's "If I Didn't Have You" from the film won for Best Song. The big moment for the two studios, though, was the showdown for Best Animated Feature, and the first-ever prize in the category went to *Shrek*. DreamWorks and Katzenberg had beaten Disney at its own game, winning the award that Walt Disney himself might have considered a "corporate birthright."

The two-page ad in *Variety* shortly thereafter underscored the importance of the award. Shrek and Fiona appeared with Shrek clutching the Oscar. "DreamWorks Pictures would like to thank the Academy of Motion Picture Arts and Sciences for awarding *Shrek* the very first Oscar for Best Animated Film." If stomachs were churning at Disney, its people might have taken solace if only they could have seen the future. DreamWorks would never again reach such heights.

10

Follow the Money

IN PROMISING to create the studio of the twenty-first century, DreamWorks's founders implied it would be tantamount to a New Deal for Hollywood. For example, early on Steven Spielberg announced that filmmakers at his studio would retain "moral rights" in their works. This would, supposedly, prevent the studio from later creating differing versions that changed the original film in order to goose more money out of the marketplace. At the time, filmmakers were complaining about distributors colorizing old black-and-white movies in what proved to be the mistaken belief that artificially colored versions would be more acceptable to modern audiences than the black-and-white originals.

Spielberg seemed to be promising that the film's creators would always have a say in the process of marketing, distribution, and preservation, long after they had moved on to other projects. This was an easy enough claim before the studio had released a single film. Jack Valenti, then head of the Motion Picture Association of America, the industry's lobbying arm, dashed cold water on the idea: "The reason the American motion picture industry is the most successful in the world is that producers can attract the capital necessary to make big movies because the producers hold all the rights."

If "moral rights" were pie in the sky, DreamWorks still had to deal with the reality of Hollywood economics, and in that it would make no significant changes. Running a studio is an immensely expensive process involving not only the cost of the individual films but the overhead involved in the entire process of production, distribution, and marketing. After the troika and outside investors (notably Paul Allen) put up the initial funds for DreamWorks, more money was needed. As Hollywood had from its inception, DreamWorks turned to the banks. Given the hype, the personalities, and the initial investors, the new studio found a warm reception. Chemical Banking Corp. headed a consortium that underwrote a $1 billion revolving credit line for DreamWorks. It's doubtful any other Hollywood start-up could have attracted such support, particularly given that repayment was over a ten-year period. The magic in the names of the founders, plus Allen's $500 million investment, proved to be irresistible.

For small investors, getting involved in Hollywood wasn't about profit but about bragging rights. You got to say you were "partners" on a particular film with the major players. For the major players, it was about making sure you got paid first. Thus as the Chemical Bank loans neared repayment, other financial institutions, like FleetBoston Financial and J. P. Morgan, were ready to make new deals. Why would they gamble on something so chancy as a future movie? At the level the financiers were operating, nothing was left to chance. All sources of income—foreign sales, home video, product licensing—were considered and part of the formula.

"With a huge database of over a million data units and our experience with over 30 films, we can predict with 95 percent accuracy how much we expect to raise from video rentals," explained Tony Hull, DreamWorks's financial whiz.

Financing an individual film can be a hugely complicated process. It's not merely writing a check to the producers who then come back with a film for the studio to distribute. To begin with, the underlying rights must be acquired. If you're making *Harry Potter and the Goblet of Fire*, you'd best have an agreement to license the movie rights to the novel from author J. K. Rowling or her successor in interest, or you may end up with a film you can't release. (This is what almost derailed the release of *Amistad*.)

Then there are the deals with the director and stars. For some films it may be a relatively simple deal: here's the money in return for your services. Bigger stars may demand tremendous amounts of money and/or a percentage of the gross. This means they will be paid from the first dollars collected at the box office and not out of "net profits," a mythical figure in Hollywood that may never be realized. "Net profits" are referred to derisively in the industry as "monkey points," since only a monkey would be stupid enough to think they are worth anything.

A sufficiently powerful director may be able to demand the right of "final cut," which means that he, not the studio, will determine the ultimate version of the film that is released. Directors with less power remain at the mercy of the studio, which can recut a film if, for example, test screenings reveal audience resistance to certain scenes, characters, or plot points. The right of final cut is something a director with a proven track record earns, or has the power to demand. It is the rare person who has final say on a studio film early in his or her career.

Once the film is released, even if it is a hit, there is no guarantee it will generate profits. After the exhibitors deduct their expenses (an arbitrary and negotiated fee that supposedly reflects the cost of operating the theater where the film is shown), studios tally up expenses: a distribution fee, interest on money expended, the costs of making prints and advertising (separate from the distribution fee), fees for distribution on home video and DVD, fees for release to cable and broadcast television, fees for merchandising, and additional deductions for gross-profit participants. The rule of thumb is that a movie must make three or four times its production cost to break even, but some movies do that and still are not profitable. The producer or director of a hit film may not like the fact that he or she is underwriting the costs of the studio's flops, but that's the way the business has worked for decades, and DreamWorks was not about to change it.

As one guide to the process notes, "If you wonder why a studio remains in business, and even prospers, remember that studios are in the distribution business. They make their living even though a film may barely break even, or even might be considered a flop." Thus if you are a participant in a film's revenue stream, you want to be paid off the top, not after various costs and expenses have been applied to what's left after the up-front people take their share.

Of course, if you are Steven Spielberg, the normal rules don't apply. For one thing, Spielberg is a name-brand director. He gets paid up front and gets his percentage off the gross, not the "monkey points" of net profits. Second, DreamWorks provided a means to cut the risk on his films. Except for his *Jurassic Park* sequel, nearly all the movies he directed during the DreamWorks era were done as co-productions with another studio, whether DreamWorks or the other studio ended up with domestic distribution rights. That meant that production costs were divided between the studios, and that receipts were similarly subject to a prearranged split. Spielberg and perhaps a star like Tom Hanks or Tom Cruise could get their money off the top. After that it was divided between the studios, where various charges were attached. A movie could earn $200 million and still not have gone into the black.

An analysis of the Spielberg/Cruise 2002 hit film *Minority Report* noted that it had taken in over $350 million in world box office and sold more than six million copies on home video. When it came time to divide up the take, Spielberg and Cruise received an estimated combined figure of at least $70 million while the two studios that had financed the film—Twentieth Century Fox and DreamWorks—realized less than $20 million apiece. While few players had the clout of Spielberg or Cruise, those who had it used it, unless they were willing to do a special small project for other reasons. For those waiting for the elusive "net profits," they might never be realized no matter how successful a movie seemed to be.

Once the movie is made, there remains the question of distribution. Not every film deserves a major theatrical release, and even the big studios will cut their losses and send a perceived clunker directly to the home-video and cable markets. For films deemed to have a chance for substantial revenues, the established studios have a well-developed system for getting them into the marketplace—from negotiating deals with exhibitors to promoting and publicizing the film to releasing it overseas, as well as handling the later release to home video and DVD. DreamWorks didn't have to reinvent the wheel releasing its films, but it did have to negotiate each step of the process and often found it more cost effective to rely on other studios to get its films out rather than carry the expense of having to finance its own distribution office.

According to one executive, a good domestic distribution operation at the time DreamWorks was starting up might run an annual budget of $15 to $20 million. "It's a lot of money if you only have a handful of pictures to release in a year," he said, and that described DreamWorks's situation exactly.

Take home video and DVD. DreamWorks was launched just as what were once called "ancillary markets" had become crucial to a film's bottom line. Many films didn't cover their initial costs until their post-theatrical life. DreamWorks might have set up its own video division, but, as we have seen, the long-term story of the studio was about shrinking its operations, not expanding. It never even tried to set up its own home-video division, instead contracting with Universal to distribute DreamWorks videos and DVDs. Because of Spielberg's long-term relationship with Universal, the deal was cozy and obvious. When the studio renewed the pact with Universal in 2001, DreamWorks realized a $250 million infusion of cash. In return, Universal held the rights to use DreamWorks characters in its theme parks. It was a mutually beneficial arrangement that nonetheless resulted in DreamWorks being a step removed from the home-video marketplace. DreamWorks received cash and a distributor, Universal got the prestige—however that might be measured—of having a deal with Katzenberg, Geffen, and especially Spielberg. DreamWorks could advise and nudge and cajole, but its home-video operations were ultimately in the hands of Universal. It worked for Dream-Works, but it was a reminder that the studio wasn't really the equal of Warner Bros. or Paramount or Twentieth Century Fox, which would never have left themselves so open to the priorities of a rival company, particularly in the domestic market.

Each step in the distribution process is an opportunity for additional revenue for a film and a chance for the company to assert itself. By the time films are ready for cable and broadcast television, the industry offers most films as part of a package. It doesn't matter if a particular movie flopped. Television outlets buy packages, not individual films, though individual titles in the package are invariably part of the draw. These ancillary releases, which may seem like afterthoughts, are in fact crucial to studios trying to maximize income on a film. Anthony Hull, chief financial officer for DreamWorks, pointed out that a film that grossed $100 million in theatrical release averaged a $237.1 million return for the studio when one included video, DVD, network, and cable licensing fees.

Foreign sales are yet another issue. Early on Dream-Works contracted with UIP, the partnership between Universal and Paramount, to handle its overseas sales. Typically the distributor takes 17 percent of film rental revenues as recompense for its efforts. Although some production companies subcontract American distribution as well, DreamWorks insisted that since it was a studio and not merely a producer of films, it would handle North American marketing for its own releases. DreamWorks believed that by controlling the film's American theatrical release, it could determine value when Universal (on home video) or UIP (on foreign sales) took the DreamWorks films farther along the pipeline. According to David Geffen, "The initial theatrical release is the locomotive that determines the film's value. We are willing to spend more money than an outside distributor would be."

The bottom line is that while making movies can be highly profitable for studios and for a handful of superstars who can demand huge fees up front and/or a percentage of gross receipts, it remains a huge roll of the dice for nearly everyone else involved in the process. For all its talk, DreamWorks did little to change that process, choosing instead to benefit from it. The studio did not rewrite the economic rules where every film has two sets of books—the financial record based on standard accounting principles, and the one where figures are determined by the studio's contractual obligations to the people involved in the film. DreamWorks's call for "moral rights" for the filmmakers did not extend to transparency in the financial aspect of the filmmaking process. In fact, given how many DreamWorks films had DreamWorks executives Walter Parkes or Laurie MacDonald as producers or executive producers (and thus entitled to up-front financial participation), the studio's "innovation" in film financing could be considered a step backward. It had come up with a new way to divert the revenue stream away from filmmakers not powerful enough to be up-front participants.

The rule at DreamWorks remained what it was at other studios: get as much money as possible before the cameras roll. If you aren't Julia Roberts or Tom Hanks or Tom Cruise or Steven Spielberg, there is no guarantee you will see any money after the fact from the film's release in theaters, DVD, overseas, or cable, no matter how much it takes in, other than the residuals negotiated by the talent guilds as part of the standard contract.

This fact would prove to be a key to DreamWorks's eventual downfall. As the studio shrank and sold off its various divisions, it came to depend more and more on revenues from film. But this part of the business involved the greatest risks with the least guarantee of substantial profits. DreamWorks's rivals could count on money from television stations, theme parks, merchandising, publishing, and other outlets, which helped keep their companies afloat until they could cash in with a big payday on a *Titanic* or a *Lord of the Rings*. DreamWorks was only as good as its next hit, and it was about to discover how precarious a position that was.

11

Catch as Catch Can

JEFFREY KATZENBERG was as pleased as he could be about *Shrek*. The critical acclaim, the box office success, the animation Oscar—it didn't get much better than this. To his credit, Katzenberg took every opportunity to remind people that the film had been a team effort. He praised not only the directors and voice cast but the numerous animators and technicians who received screen credit but won little fame or glory. He could afford to be magnanimous. After the disappointment of *Prince of Egypt* and the failure of *Road to El Dorado*, the success of *Shrek* was his vindication. He had beaten Disney not only in the courtroom but where it really mattered, on the big screen. In the early months of 2002, DreamWorks could easily coast.

While the K of SKG took his bows, where were the other two partners? David Geffen's name rarely appeared in news of DreamWorks any more, except to remind people he was part of the troika. He was said to be negotiating deals behind the scenes and in constant contact with Katzenberg and Spielberg, but if someone read about Geffen in 2002 it would be far removed from Hollywood. It might be his listing in the top one hundred of *Forbes* magazine's ranking of the wealthiest Americans. It might be his charitable work, like his $200 million endowment for the UCLA Medical School. Or it might be the increasingly negative press about his fighting public access to the beach bordering his Malibu home, or the silly and false rumors that Geffen—who was now openly gay—was involved with, or had even married, the actor Keanu Reeves. What one didn't see were stories about Geffen signing up artists or planning promotional campaigns or engaging in his legendary deal-making for DreamWorks's music division. He may have been in touch with the people running it, but his active days in the music world seemed to be behind him.

As for Spielberg, after the triumph of *Saving Private Ryan* and the debacle of *A.I.*, he had been busy making money—for himself and for other studios. Although the miniseries *Band of Brothers* was a DreamWorks project and had done well on HBO, on the big screen moviegoers were more likely to see Spielberg's name as executive producer for *Jurassic Park III* for Universal or for *Men in Black II* for Columbia. Perhaps it was out of a sense of guilt, or more likely the realization that his name would be a good marketing tool, that the 2002 Sci-Fi Channel miniseries Dream-Works produced was prominently promoted as *Steven Spielberg Presents "Taken."* More important, Spielberg was hard at work on two blockbuster films, one of which would be released through Twentieth Century Fox and the other through DreamWorks. Both *Minority Report*, which was a DreamWorks partnership with Twentieth, and *Catch Me If You Can*, which was a pure DreamWorks film, would do exceptionally well at the box office. But it was fair to ask why Spielberg was doing work for other studios at all. Both *Jurassic Park* and *Men in Black* were properties that pre-dated DreamWorks, yet it remained odd to see Spielberg devoting time to enriching the competition. It seemed even odder since Walter Parkes and Laurie MacDonald were also involved in *Men in Black II*. This sequel ended up earning $425 million worldwide. Why would DreamWorks be happy with its three top film people producing a blockbuster project for a rival studio? Shouldn't they have been spending their time developing such projects for DreamWorks?

Instead DreamWorks kicked off 2002 with a remake of H. G. Wells's *The Time Machine*. Perhaps the most interesting thing about it was that director Simon Wells, who had co-directed *Prince of Egypt*, was the author's great-grandson. Walter Parkes, who produced the film with David Valdes, paid homage to the 1960 film by George Pal but noted, "Today, we have technologies that allow us to recreate a world as imagined by H. G. Wells in ways they couldn't, which is exciting." Audiences didn't think so. The film made less than $60 million in the United States and an anemic $38 million overseas. On an estimated $80 million budget, it was a loss.

If the preceding two years were any guide, DreamWorks would come alive in the summer, whether with adult fare like *Saving Private Ryan* or family fun like *Shrek*, and since Spielberg's *Minority Report* belonged to Twentieth Century Fox domestically, the DreamWorks lineup consisted of new films from Woody Allen, Sam Mendes (fresh off his Oscar win for *American Beauty*), and a new animated offering that would once again set the standard for the form.

The season began with great fanfare when DreamWorks premiered Allen's *Hollywood Ending* and the animated *Spirit: Stallion of the Cimarron* at the Cannes Film Festival in advance of stateside release. Allen, no longer so reticent about doing publicity, came to Cannes for the first time to push his film. *Spirit* was shown out of competition but with plenty of hoopla: an outdoor screening accompanied by live performances of the music for the film by Bryan Adams and the composer of the film's score, Hans Zimmer. Noted *Variety*, "In just five years of theatrical releasing, the company has displayed uncommon savvy at using film fests such as Cannes and Toronto to launch successful pics." In earlier years *American Beauty* had premiered in Toronto and *Shrek* had kicked off at Cannes, creating much higher profiles for the films than would have been achieved simply by putting them into general release.

The premiere for *Hollywood Ending* led to a cascade of publicity for the film. Allen was awarded the *Palme des Palmes*, a prize given to honor his entire career. A grateful Allen thanked the festival audience and then said he was going out to get something to eat while they saw the movie since he didn't like watching his own work. The movie itself featured Allen as a director who had once been a great film-maker but had fallen on hard times. He gets a break to do one more feature but grows so nervous and hysterical that—for no organic reason—he goes temporarily blind. The "joke" of the movie is that he attempts to direct the film anyway. Allen had taken a throwaway gag from his 1977 *Annie Hall*, when his character became nauseated before doing an award show and miraculously recovered when he was replaced—and attempted to inflate it into a feature-length movie. It was no doubt appreciated at Cannes because the punch line of the film is that the blind director's movie flops upon release but is hailed as a work of genius in France.

Critics divided between those who liked *Hollywood Ending* and those who said it marked the end of Allen's own career. Allen had never been a maker of blockbusters, but he usually had strong critical support and a core audience that eagerly anticipated each new film. It's why he was able to retain his independence even as he moved from studio to studio. He made films on a tight (but not small) budget and had a sufficient worldwide following to guarantee those films would be profitable. *Hannah and Her Sisters* made only $40 million in domestic box office when it was released in 1986, and was considered successful. *Hollywood Ending*, costing an economical $16 million, didn't even earn $5 million in the United States. The new Woody Allen films were no longer being anticipated by his fans; they were being dreaded.

At Cannes, Allen was the center of attention of events for *Hollywood Ending* while the DreamWorks people stayed in the background. For *Spirit*, though, Jeffrey Katzenberg was front and center. He explained that the film would be shown with live music for its entire running time, even though the studio had tested it that way with only a few scenes. "We had to do a first," said Katzenberg. It wasn't enough merely to come back to Cannes with another animated feature. It had to be an event. Bryan Adams joked that the song "Get Off My Back" was inspired by all the input he had been getting about the lyrics from Katzenberg, who had advised him to be metaphorical, not descriptive. Already thinking ahead, Katzenberg also plugged the 2003 release of *Sinbad*, suggesting that if he could find another "first" he'd love to premiere that film at Cannes too. Katzenberg made it clear that his personal focus as a studio head was on animation, and that he expected the great works in the field to come from DreamWorks. In his view of film history, animation was seeing another "renaissance," following the previous rebirth at Disney in the late 1980s and early 1990s.

Spirit is the story of a horse who is captured in turn by soldiers and by an Indian but yearns to be free. Unlike other cartoon animals he doesn't speak, but we hear his "thoughts" voiced by Matt Damon. To help animators understand his character, Katzenberg claimed to have told them to look to Bruce Willis in the *Die Hard* films, and he even screened the first of those action movies several times for them. He wanted them to note the character's optimism and his refusal to give up no matter how bad things got. Katzenberg started referring to the project as *Spirit: Die Horse*.

Of course it wasn't just about the character's toughness. "Horses are among the most beloved and beautiful creatures on the planet," said Katzenberg. "I loved the idea of an animated movie about horses, but I know there is no animal more difficult to animate." The resulting film was indeed beautiful to look at. Although it was done largely as hand-drawn traditional animation, the film also used computer graphics animation throughout, not only for background locations but even for some of the lead characters. Katzenberg tried to coin a new word for this mixture of old and new animation: "tradigital." He had high hopes for the film, even arranging for the studio to buy a Kiger mustang in order to have a readily accessible model for the artists who were animating the horse characters. To ensure a consistency between the drawn and computer-animated characters, some of the animators were trained so they could handle both techniques. Doug Cooper, the film's digital supervisor, predicted, "I think we're going to see more painterly and stylistic 3D films. As the technology is blending, so too are the creative styles."

Even the storytelling technique for *Spirit* was radically different. Although the human characters speak, much of the story is told visually, with songs or narration expressing feelings instead of advancing the plot. To get the look of the

Western landscape, Katzenberg, co-directors Kelly Asbury and Lorna Cook, and several members of the production team went on a field trip, covering eight national parks in four days including Yosemite, Yellowstone, Grand Teton, and the Grand Canyon. The resulting film was stunning, with the cartoon horses acting like real horses and yet with incredible expression, set against backdrops that were recognizable to those familiar with the real-life settings such as Monument Valley, where John Ford had shot many of his classic Westerns. It was a stirring tribute to the spirit of freedom, and in spite of the clumsy secondary title of *Stallion of the Cimarron*, Katzenberg and his DreamWorks team had every reason to be proud of the completed work. They had accomplished what they set out to do.

There was just one problem. As with *Prince of Egypt* and *Road to El Dorado*, no one seems to have asked if there was an audience for the movie. Although youngsters seemed to like it, it was a serious (i.e., not cartoony) film, yet it had no unorthodox romance or star voice cast to draw in adults. Matt Damon was a well-regarded actor, but there didn't seem to be many people who would pay to hear his voice rendering a horse's thoughts. The film cost an estimated $80 million, opened strongly with some $23 million, but then went downhill fast. It finished at $73 million, with another $33 million worldwide. Perhaps, in the long run, with video and DVD and cable, it would turn a profit, but *Spirit* was no *Shrek*.

Four years later Katzenberg still stood by *Spirit*, though he acknowledged it had been a risky undertaking. "I still look at *Spirit* and feel that it's one of the most ambitious animated movies that I've been involved in over the last 25 years. It was like Butch and Sundance going off the cliff and hoping to heck there's water down there," he told an interviewer in 2006. "But I have to say that artistically, I could put that movie on today and just be spellbound by it."

Katzenberg may remain proud, but in 2002 *Spirit* was considered a letdown after the phenomenal success of *Shrek*. To add insult to injury, Disney's summer animated release, *Lilo & Stitch*, was a smash hit. It too broke the mold in some ways, with audiences responding to an out-of-control space alien who develops a fondness for Elvis Presley and finds a home with two orphaned sisters on Earth. It surpassed *Spirit*'s grosses in its first four weeks of release and went on to earn more than $145 million in domestic box office alone, then adding another $117 million overseas.

Katzenberg insisted he wasn't comparing DreamWorks to Disney. Shortly before *Spirit* was released, he told an interviewer, "If our movies were coming out a week or two apart from one another then you could say we directly compete, but we don't. *Spirit*'s success or failure will not be impacted by how well *Lilo & Stitch* does or doesn't do. And vice versa. So I wish them well. I'm rooting for them. I'd rather they have *another* animated movie be a blockbuster out there. That's good news. The more these movies succeed, the more it expands the market, the more the moviegoers look forward to these films."

Time would tell if *Shrek* or *Spirit* was the aberration for DreamWorks, but now the hope for saving the summer rested in a dark gangster film from *American Beauty* director Sam Mendes. *Road to Perdition* asked an interesting question: Would American audiences accept nice guy Tom Hanks as a hit man?

"DreamWorks keeps making its own rules and then breaking them," wrote one reporter. "It consistently refuses to pigeonhole itself while it taps into disparate creative energies."

Still riding the crest of success, the news in 2002 was that DreamWorks was now in the black. Bonuses had been paid out to some employees, a first. Of course because the company was privately held, there was no way to confirm details. *Variety* relied on sources who had had access to the DreamWorks books during merger talks that had taken place with different studios and production companies. They quoted Jessica Reif Cohen of the investment firm of Merrill, Lynch, who said, "I am impressed by their numbers. Sure they had their losses, like everyone, but they're shrewd and they're tough and they quickly cut their losses on ventures that clearly aren't working for them." Thus the Pop.com disaster was taken as a plus. It wasn't working, so they ditched it rather than sending good money after bad. It was also pointed out that even on films with less than spectacular box office runs, like *Evolution* and *Almost Famous*, the back ends of these co-ventures—sales of DVDs, cable, pay-per-view, etc.—had together brought in more than $100 million of revenue. Katzenberg boasted, "This company is entrepreneurial, not corporate. We feel the need to push boundaries."

One way to do that was to engage in summer counter-programming. Summer was a time for smash hits, comic book superheroes, teen comedies, and the like. DreamWorks had released *Saving Private Ryan* in the summer of 1998 to great success since it was one of the few movies for grown-ups in the theaters. Now they would try to do it again with another Tom Hanks movie, *The Road to Perdition*.

Directed by Sam Mendes and loosely based on a graphic novel of the same name, *Road to Perdition* was a dark meditation on fathers and sons set against the world of organized crime in depression-era Chicago. A mustachioed Hanks played Michael Sullivan, a gunman loyal to mob boss John Rooney (Paul Newman), who treats him as a son. Rooney's own son Connor (Daniel Craig) is somewhat out of control, shooting when he should stand down, and skimming money from his father's ill-gotten gains. Sullivan and Connor are on a collision course, ending in the death of Sullivan's wife and younger son, and forcing Rooney to side with his own flesh and blood. Sullivan and his older boy, Michael Jr. (Tyler Hoechlin), are soon on the run. Sullivan wants to protect his son, but he also wants to hit Rooney where it hurts, and he begins robbing Rooney's operations, which he knows all too well. The mob can't afford this sort of civil war and brings in an outside hit man (Jude Law) to take out Sullivan.

Some critics found the plot a bit schematic, with the two sets of fathers and sons playing off the "like a son" relationship between Rooney and Sullivan. But Mendes and cinematographer Conrad L. Hall (in what would be his final feature film before his death in January 2003) succeeded in creating a vision of the Midwest in the 1930s that was starkly beautiful. The final confrontation between Sullivan and Rooney is almost operatic as two men who have loved each other find themselves—almost against their wills—on opposite sides, meeting on a city street in the pouring rain in what they know will inevitably mean the end of one of their lives. Indeed, though the usual references to *The Godfather* were trotted out in some reviews, *Road to Perdition* was the first gangster movie in three decades that clearly owed nothing to Francis Ford Coppola's mobster classic. *The Godfather* was about a crime family against the rest of the world. *Road to Perdition* was about two fathers wanting to provide for their sons, and the price they pay for it. Sullivan, in spite of naming his son for himself, doesn't want Michael Jr. following in his footsteps. He wants the sins of the father to end with himself. Said Mendes, "That is the core of the story: two men protecting their children. In the end, what can be more important than that?"

Road to Perdition had great performances by Hanks and Newman, among others, and proved to be a major contribution to one of the most American of genres, the gangster film. There was the rub: audiences could go for a grown-up movie in the summer, but there was a big difference between *Saving Private Ryan* and *Road to Perdition*. The former had lots of action but was essentially a positive story. In spite of the fact that several of the characters die, most viewers left the theater cheered by the heroism of the "greatest generation" and thrilled by the battle scenes. *Perdition* was a darker, moodier film, with its happy ending consisting of Sullivan's son surviving the carnage but little else in the way of an upbeat message. According to Mendes, "With *Perdition* there are two layers. First, there's a subtle, complex layer about violence and redemption and the secret life our parents lead that we never really know about. That's the secret movie. Then there's the other movie, which is a more conventional narrative about fathers and sons."

Either way it was a tough sell, but it was a movie that might have thrived had it been released as the year's Oscar contender in November or December. It could have opened in just a few locations in December to qualify for the Oscars and then gone wider in January. Serious films do well in the fall and winter.

DreamWorks, though, had Steven Spielberg's *Catch Me If You Can* as its big holiday release (a movie that, ironically, could have done great business in the summer). Even assuming it could have been ready by late July, they were not about to put it up against Spielberg's own *Minority Report*, which had opened the month before. The Dream-Works schedule was convenient for Spielberg but did not necessarily let the studio play to its strengths. *Catch Me* might also have been pushed back to 2003. It couldn't be released near *Road to Perdition* since it also featured Hanks, and it wouldn't make sense to have him competing with himself in two DreamWorks movies. But if delayed it would have to wait until the following summer, since a Spielberg movie was a "tent pole" film around which a studio built the rest of its release schedule. Since *Jaws*, a Spielberg movie opened either for the summer or for the holiday season, never in March or October.

Terry Press, the DreamWorks publicity chief, tried to put the best spin on things when handicapping the Oscars in December. "Look at how many movies are out now. I don't know if we would be over $100 million [in U.S. box office receipts] had we put it out now. To be the only adult choice in July and August benefited the movie."

Maybe so, but *Road to Perdition* barely topped $100 million in domestic box office and took in $57 million in foreign returns. It wasn't a flop, but it wasn't a megahit either, and this was a major problem for the studio. In the first eight months of 2002 it had released four films. *The Time Machine* and *Hollywood Ending* were essentially dead on arrival, but *Spirit* and *Road to Perdition* were solid, well-crafted, and well-received films that, for whatever reason, didn't become cultural phenomena as *Saving Private Ryan*, *American Beauty*, *Gladiator*, and *Shrek* had. This was DreamWorks's wake-up call. Given the hundreds of movies released each year, it's obvious that most films don't turn

into "must sees" that everyone talks about and some viewers see more than once. Most studios would have been relatively happy with the box office returns on *Spirit* and
Road. Financially DreamWorks would have to share the returns on *Road* with Twentieth Century Fox, but that studio
would be sharing the much larger returns ($358 million
worldwide) on *Minority Report* with DreamWorks. The difference is that, as discussed in the preceding chapter, for
DreamWorks this was pretty much it. Twentieth Century
Fox was part of Rupert Murdoch's empire, including news-
papers, book publishing, a television network, ownership of
a large number of local stations, several cable channels, and
numerous other enterprises. Disney could rely on its theme
parks, television network and cable channels, publishing,
and other merchandising. Columbia was part of Sony, one
of the world's largest electronics concerns. Warners was
part of the Time-Warner media conglomerate which included magazines, television production, a mini-network
(the WB), and many other enterprises.

Having sold off its interactive division and given up pursuing a syndicated television niche, the world of Dream-
Works was shrinking, and would continue to shrink further.
This was a studio that needed big hits every year or else had
to start releasing many more movies, hoping to make up in
volume where it fell short on blockbusters. That was how
most successful studios worked, with anywhere from a
dozen to two dozen movies released each year—often
through different divisions—so that the success of the enterprise didn't depend on any one film being the next *Gladiator* or *Shrek*.

DreamWorks would have only three more at bats in
2002.

The Tuxedo was exactly the sort of basic action comedy that studios toss out like popcorn. It wasn't a prestige film, but on a schedule of twenty movies it would serve its function and no one would think twice about it. As one of only two fall releases from DreamWorks, it was a bit of an embarrassment. It starred Jackie Chan, a popular international action and comedy star, but like the deal with Woody Allen, DreamWorks was getting someone past his prime. Chan remained an engaging on-screen presence, but as an action star he was pushing fifty and was no longer able (or perhaps was unwilling) to do some of the amazing acrobatic stuntwork from his earlier days. One of the highlights of a Chan film used to be the outtakes during the closing credits, where you could see him fall or get banged up. The message was always clear: it really was the actor doing those death-defying leaps and other stunts, and sometimes he missed. With *The Tuxedo*, Chan's stunts were now enhanced with computer graphic special effects, and they weren't quite the same. The film pulled in $50 million in the United States, and couldn't match even that overseas. It would prove to be little more than a throwaway September release, quickly shoved out of the way for other films and sent off to DVD and cable.

The surprise on the schedule turned out to be *The Ring*. Although most of the American filmgoing public remained unaware, a number of new Japanese directors of horror films had developed their own style and sensibility. The films were eerie and created a dark and unsettling mood. This new wave was dubbed "J-horror" and had played mostly in art houses in the United States. That was about to change with *The Ring*, a remake of a 1998 Japanese hit called *Ringu*. Produced by Walter Parkes and Laurie Mac-

Donald, the remake might not have satisfied Japanese audiences, but it was different than anything most American viewers had seen. It starred Naomi Watts (fresh off her star-making turn in *Mulholland Drive*) as a reporter investigating stories about a weird video. People who watch it and its strange, unexplained images receive a phone call telling them they will die in seven days. A group of teenagers watch the video and die, and so the reporter covering the story now feels she must solve the mystery before she dies too. When her young son mistakenly views the tape, she has an added reason to prevent the curse from being fulfilled. As with *Gladiator*, DreamWorks was out first with what would prove to be a trendsetting film.

Mark Sourian, an executive at DreamWorks, saw *Ringu* and brought it to the attention of Parkes and MacDonald. According to Parkes, "Mark said, 'I've just seen the scariest movie in my life. You have to see it right away.' Laurie and I cancelled everything and watched the movie. . . . We were both frightened and mesmerized by it, and immediately decided we were going to remake the movie." Mainstream critics were mixed—as they often are about horror films—but audiences were not. The film grossed $229 million worldwide, which was phenomenal for a horror film that had cost only $45 million. By comparison, none of the *Scream* films came close to the $200 million mark. Here was the big hit DreamWorks needed, but in spite of the seriousness of the production and a top-flight cast, *The Ring* was not the sort of movie that won Oscars. The bank may not have cared if the money flowing into DreamWorks accounts came from *Road to Perdition* or from *The Ring*, but for status-conscious Hollywood there was a big difference.

Of course, *The Ring* didn't end up empty-handed. It seems every successful movie ends up winning some sort of prize, and *The Ring* received such awards as the Saturn (best actress for Naomi Watts from the Academy of Science Fiction, Fantasy & Horror Films, USA), the Golden Trailer, and an MTV Movie Award for best villain (Daveigh Chase, who played the dead child in the cursed video). These kudos were no doubt satisfying for their recipients, but they didn't mean added dollars at the box office or greater prestige for DreamWorks.

Instead the studio was hoping that Oscar lightning would strike a third time with *Road to Perdition*. *Variety* noted that historically 86 percent of all nominations for Best Picture at the Oscars had been released in November or December, yet *Gladiator* had been a May release, *Saving Private Ryan* came out in July, and *American Beauty* had opened in September. Why couldn't *Road to Perdition* succeed?

First, though, was the Christmas Day release of the year's second Spielberg movie, *Catch Me If You Can*. This was Spielberg in a lighter, playful mood. It was a grown-up film as opposed to one of his amusement park rides like *Jurassic Park*, but the focus of the story was Frank W. Abagnale. He was a real-life person who had successfully impersonated a doctor, a lawyer, and an airline pilot, and who financed his spree with forged checks, eventually being brought to justice by the FBI. Abagnale—who was subsequently convicted, did his time, and then went straight earning a living as a security expert—proved to be an engaging movie character as portrayed by Leonardo DiCaprio. Set in the early 1960s, Spielberg and his production played off both the color and the innocence of the era, filling the soundtrack with period pop tunes and the screen with colorful sixties fashions. It helped to have both DiCaprio and Tom Hanks (as a composite of the FBI agents who pursued Abagnale) as well as a supporting cast that included Christopher Walken, Martin Sheen, Nathalie Baye, Amy Adams, and Jennifer Garner. It proved to be another hit for the studio, taking in nearly $340 million worldwide and allowing DreamWorks to end a disappointing year on an upbeat note.

Walter Parkes refused to be discouraged. "It was a good solid year. *The Ring* left everyone on a big high." In fact it was a mediocre year with three flops, two disappointing but okay summer releases, and two solid fourth-quarter hits. Unlike past years, though, there was little validation at Oscar time. *Road to Perdition* was not nominated for Best Picture. All five nominees were films that had been released in the final two weeks of the year.

Road received six nominations, with Paul Newman leading the way with a nod for supporting actor. The only winner was a posthumous one, with the late Conrad L. Hall winning for his cinematography. His son, Conrad W. Hall, accepted the Oscar in his place; for a movie about fathers and sons, it was somehow fitting. *Catch Me If You Can* received two nominations, with Christopher Walken up for supporting actor for his well-regarded turn as Leonard DiCaprio's father, but the film was shut out. This was the year of *The Pianist* and *Chicago*.

DreamWorks's slim hopes for a major Oscar victory were dashed when the second Oscar for Best Animated Feature was named. *Spirit* had been nominated; the computer-animated *Ice Age*, from Twentieth Century Fox, had been too. The other three slots in the newly expanded category went to Disney releases: the hit *Lilo & Stitch*, the flop *Treasure Planet*, and the film that won—and which Disney had had nothing to do with except acquiring it for American release—*Spirited Away*, by Japanese master animator Hayao Miyazaki.

The year 2002 was just so-so for DreamWorks. Its people having convinced themselves they were rewriting the rules, they found that the rest of the world wasn't necessarily going along. If the people at the top had been paying attention, they might have learned and adapted. Instead they were about to discover that things could get a lot worse.

12

Taking Stock

IN HOLLYWOOD, as the saying goes, you're only as good as your last film. For motion picture studios it might be adapted: a company is only as good as its latest slate of releases. DreamWorks had only six films scheduled to open in 2003, of which only one came anywhere near being considered successful. The total domestic box office for DreamWorks movies released over the course of the year was $128.3 million—for the studio's *entire* slate.

Little time need be spent on the films themselves. *Biker Boyz*—$21.7 million gross—demonstrated that not even an impressive cast headed by Laurence Fishburne could lure audiences into an African-American motorcycle movie. *Head of State*—$37.8 million—confirmed a similar lack of demand for starring vehicles with comedian Chris Rock. *Anything Else*—$3.2 million—showed that even Woody Allen's hard-core fans were giving up on him; the film was even more embarrassing than *Hollywood Ending*. The holiday release of *House of Sand and Fog*—$13 million—helped launch an American career for the talented Iranian actress Shoreh Aghdashloo, but not even stars Ben Kingsley and Jennifer Connelly could attract moviegoers to this tragedy of an Iranian family and a hapless woman fighting over a house.

As for the big summer animated release of *Sinbad: Legend of the Seven Seas*, Jeffrey Katzenberg had called it "our attempt to do an homage to Steven Spielberg. It is meant to be *Indiana Jones* in animation." But an animated film could take three or four years to produce, and by 2003 it was pretty well established that American moviegoers wanted their cartoons to be funny and that boys in particular had no interest in animated adventure. *Road to El Dorado*, *Titan A.E.*, *Atlantis: The Lost Empire*, and *Treasure Planet* had all failed, and even *Spirit* had not met expectations.

In DreamWorks fashion, the voice cast of *Sinbad* was heavily promoted. Brad Pitt, Catherine Zeta-Jones, and Michelle Pfeiffer were the big guns, with Joseph Fiennes and Dennis Haysbert on board as well. The film had a script by John Logan, who shared the Oscar nomination for the *Gladiator* screenplay. Like *Spirit*, it turned out to be a well-crafted film without an audience. It took in only $26.3 million domestically, but additional overseas box office boosted it to $43.2 million, making it the studio's second-biggest film of the year.

Ann Daly, head of the animation unit, confessed, "We are extremely disappointed." Her boss, Katzenberg, went further, taking the opportunity of *Sinbad*'s failure to announce that DreamWorks would no longer do cel animation. "I think the idea of a traditional story being told using traditional animation is likely a thing of the past," he said.

As if to ensure DreamWorks's complete humiliation, Disney released its own animated ocean adventure that summer, the Pixar-produced *Finding Nemo*, which would become the most successful animated feature to date. Its

U.S. receipts alone—$339.7 million—eclipsed Dream-Works's entire release schedule. *Nemo* would go on to earn more than $500 million overseas for a grand total of $865 million. As of this writing it is eleventh on the list of all-time box office champs.

Only one DreamWorks film could be called anything close to successful, and it was one of the least likely prospects, a goofy comedy called *Old School*. Vince Vaughn, Luke Wilson, and Will Ferrell starred as three thirty-somethings who don't like having to be grown-ups and try to recapture their youth by opening a fraternity where they can make their own rules. One of the executive producers was Ivan Reitman, who had produced the obvious forebear to the film, the 1978 hit *Animal House*. A generation too far removed from the seventies (not to mention the early sixties, when *Animal House* was set) embraced *Old School* as its own. Vaughn, who had been floundering by being miscast in dramatic clunkers like *Domestic Disturbance* and *Return to Paradise*, soared as the married family man let loose in fraternity life. Will Ferrell had gained a following on television's *Saturday Night Live* but had not yet scored on film. *Old School* provided a significant boost. The third member of the trio was Luke Wilson, a light leading man who already had a following from appearing in the films of cult director Wes Anderson (*Bottle Rocket, Rushmore, The Royal Tenenbaums*). It was a broad, silly film, and it found its audience to the tune of $74.6 million. It wasn't a blockbuster, but it was the best a Dream-Works release would do that year.

What went wrong? Spielberg himself offered the pat explanation that it was just the luck of the draw: "This is our first shitty year." Walter Parkes tried another tack, suggesting they knew all along they didn't have much to offer in

2003: "This is a transitional year for us. It's a cycle. When you're busy producing, your development always suffers."

In fact Parkes and his wife Laurie MacDonald had been very busy producing instead of attending to their day jobs at DreamWorks. Parkes was listed as executive producer or producer on no less than seven movies in 2002, when he might have been working on getting more product in the pipeline for 2003. These included DreamWorks releases *The Time Machine*, *Road to Perdition*, *The Tuxedo*, *The Ring*, and *Catch Me If You Can*, as well as *Men in Black II* and *Minority Report*, movies released in the United States by other studios, though DreamWorks had been a partner on *Minority Report*. Five of those films also listed MacDonald as producer or executive producer. Spielberg was off directing. Katzenberg was focusing on animation. Geffen was barely involved in day-to-day operations. The chief person minding the store was new production chief Michael DeLuca (who answered to all of them), and he could only offer boiler-plate excuses: "Studios can overreact when their films don't work. But the game plan at DreamWorks really works." Added MacDonald, "Our development drives our distribution, not the other way around."

Since DreamWorks was not publicly traded, it did not have to answer to stockholders, and Parkes and MacDonald's obvious conflict of interest was not open to challenge as long as it was okay with the principals. Said Parkes, "It's not difficult to manage this situation inside DreamWorks. What seems to be difficult is managing the perception of our arrangement." Parkes even tried to spin DreamWorks's weak year as a positive thing. "We can afford to have a thin year," he said. "A thin year is preferable to one filled with big-budget failures." (This statement would prove prophetic after the release of the big-budget failure of *The*

Island in 2005.) Instead, big-budget films were left to other studios, sometimes with DreamWorks as a partner. The studio was a partner with Universal on *Seabiscuit* and with Paramount on the horrendous travesty of Dr. Seuss's *The Cat in the Hat*. They represented additional revenue streams for DreamWorks, but they were not a substitute for its own releases. As *Variety*'s Peter Bart put it, recalling the original promise that DreamWorks would make distinctive films, "The films emerging from DreamWorks . . . are essentially indistinguishable from those of any other studio, except for the fact that there are fewer of them."

Part of the problem was that DreamWorks refused to green-light a film until all its elements were lined up. DeLuca was able to okay *Biker Boyz* and *Old School* because they were lower-budgeted films. *The Terminal* and *Collateral*, both of which were released in 2004, were held up until Tom Hanks was signed to the former and Tom Cruise and director Michael Mann were signed to the latter.

On the animation side, it was clear that DreamWorks was ending its commitment to hand-drawn animation. For all the talk about *Spirit* representing a blending of traditional and digital styles, the studio decided that computer animation was the future. *Shrek 2*, *Shark Tale*, *Madagascar*, and the television series *Father of the Pride* would all be computer animated.

On the live-action side, though, DreamWorks's schedule remained a confusing mess. The studio that had once promised to build a family of writers to develop projects on which they would share in gross profits, now was looking for package deals. Nonetheless Spielberg still called the shots on the live-action side while retaining full confidence in Parkes and MacDonald. "The greatest contribution I've made to DreamWorks is bringing Walter and Laurie with me," said the director. This was not a widely held opinion outside the studio, where some filmmakers complained that Parkes was attaching himself to the most appealing projects as producer. Indeed, it was reported that Parkes told agents to send good material direct to him and Mac-Donald, turning the DreamWorks development system—in the eyes of its critics—into looking for movies for Parkes and MacDonald to produce. According to one producer, "They're very cheap and they work at a snail's pace and they don't pay attention to them if they're not Walter's projects."

Being named producer of a film isn't simply about screen credit or approval over other elements of the film. It's also about money, with a producer credit being worth up to 5 percent of the revenue on a given movie. For *The Ring*, for example, Parkes and MacDonald collected some $4 million as producers, quite apart from any salary from DreamWorks. For his part, Spielberg felt they earned these extra rewards. "I want them to be comfortable and happy," he said, making it clear he felt they had earned this for their work at the studio.

Amidst all the complaints about DreamWorks's pathetic 2003 lineup and whose fault it was, a larger issue loomed. The studio had lined up new financing and was planning to increase its animation output to two or three films per year. An increase in live-action production was also promised. Regardless of how that worked out, DreamWorks faced a deadline. Paul Allen, who had put up a sizable amount of the money that launched DreamWorks, would soon be entitled to start cashing out. He was first in line to recover what had grown to a $670 million investment and then to see 24.5 percent of any money over $1 billion when the studio was sold or otherwise began distribution of its profits. DreamWorks insisted it would not be sold and had no desire to go public. It could only hope that 2004 would bring better news, and that a sequel to *Shrek* would make everyone forget 2003.

The first few months of 2004 seemed like more of the same. The mildly amusing romantic comedy *Win a Date with Tad Hamilton* (in which the engaging young cast of Kate Bosworth, Topher Grace, and Josh Duhamel struggled with lightweight material) grossed only $17 million. *Eurotrip*, an attempt to capitalize on the success of *Road Trip* and *Old School*, similarly fizzled at $17.7 million. Then there was *Envy*, a Barry Levinson comedy originally set for release in 2003, about Ben Stiller becoming envious of his friend Jack Black when Black's character gets rich from inventing a spray to deal with dog poop. A career low for all involved, it took in only $12.2 million. Clearly these were not the movies that would turn DreamWorks around.

Instead hopes were pinned on *Shrek 2*, and not just for box office revenue. Although publicly denying it, DreamWorks had quietly lined up the investment firms of Goldman Sachs and J. P. Morgan Chase to valuate the studio's animation unit. *Business Week* reported in May that DreamWorks was "counting on a blockbuster *Shrek 2* to help launch plans for an IPO of its animation unit later this year."

Katzenberg had planned on a *Shrek* sequel while the first film was still in production. "I felt we had only told part of the story. I felt it was incomplete," he said, suggesting that Princess Fiona's backstory—her family and her relationship with Prince Charming—were yet to be told.

Mike Myers, Cameron Diaz, and Eddie Murphy returned from the first film's voice cast and were joined by

Julie Andrews, John Cleese, Jennifer Saunders, Rupert Everett, and—nearly stealing the film—Antonio Banderas as Puss in Boots, a swashbuckling cat who had to pause to cough up the occasional hairball. (DreamWorks later announced that the cat would get his own film in 2008.) Although losing the element of surprise, as almost always happens with sequels, *Shrek 2* managed to avoid the trap of simply being the first film, only louder. The malicious fairy godmother—who wanted Princess Fiona for her own son instead of Shrek—proved to be a new and interesting villain, while the addition of Puss in Boots provided an additional and very different comic foil for Donkey.

Shrek 2 became not merely a hit but a phenomenon. It earned $100 million at the box office just on opening weekend. Even if it was the three-day Memorial Day Weekend, that was major. Jim Tharp, head of distribution for DreamWorks, professed to be "astounded," saying, "We thought we would get in the 70s for the weekend and we hoped to get to the 80s. It's playing exceptionally at every level." To put this into context, the movie had topped $260 million by the end of its second weekend. That same weekend Mel Gibson's controversial hit film *The Passion of the Christ* was at a cumulative gross of almost $370 million—and it had been playing for four months. The new *Shrek* would eventually surpass *Finding Nemo* to become the biggest animated hit ever. As of this writing it stands as the seventh highest-grossing film of all time, with $436.5 in American box office receipts and an additional $466 overseas—a total of $902.5 million. If Katzenberg and his partners wanted an advertisement to entice people to invest in DreamWorks Animation, they couldn't have made a greater impact unless they sent Spielberg door to door, inviting them to buy stock.

Katzenberg now spoke in interviews of at least two more *Shrek* sequels as well as two to three animated films each year. Later that fall the studio opened *Shark Tale*, with a voice cast that included Will Smith, Robert DeNiro, Renée Zellweger, Angelina Jolie, and movie director Martin Scorsese. Already on tap for 2005 was *Madagascar* and the next clay-animation epic from Nick Park, *Wallace and Gromit in the Curse of the Were-Rabbit*. Now that the failures of *Spirit* and *Sinbad* were past, and he was being hailed as the man who had helped shepherd two *Shrek* films to the screen, Katzenberg grew expansive. While not trying to claim credit for the work of others, he seemed to be happy that at long last he had found a Hollywood domain he could call his own.

"I love making animation movies," he gushed to one interviewer. "For my part, it's why I wanted to start DreamWorks—to be able to continue to do something that I fell in love with in my ten years at Disney. The opportunity to work with some of the most brilliant and talented people in the business—storytellers and designers and actors and writers who make these films—is really the thing that makes me happiest, the thing I enjoy the most." No one was more surprised at this than Katzenberg himself, who recalled starting at Disney without having the first clue about how to run an animation studio. "I arrived at Disney in 1984, and somebody pointed out the animation building to me and said, 'That's your problem.' Why and how I came to fall in love with it—have this attraction to it—I have no idea. It's like when you meet your perfect mate. Who can explain why? It's chemistry."

As 2004 progressed, things brightened at DreamWorks. The music division was sold off. The TV side achieved a modest hit as part of its NBC deal with the launch of the series *Las Vegas*.

On the film side, things were shakier. Spielberg's third team-up with Tom Hanks, the fey comedy *The Terminal*, proved not to be a charm. It was the story of an Eastern European man trapped in the international lounge of a New York airport when a coup in his homeland renders his passport worthless. Its $77 million in domestic box office was a hit for a low-budget comedy like *Old School* but a flop when applied to a Spielberg/Hanks film with an estimated cost of $60 million.

On the other hand, the $84 million domestic gross was quite respectable for *Anchorman: The Legend of Ron Burgundy*, a broad Will Ferrell spoof about television news that cost only a reported $26 million. *Collateral* was a tough and stylish thriller directed by Michael Mann about a cab driver (Jamie Foxx) doing the bidding of a coldhearted hit man (Tom Cruise, playing his first out-and-out villain). It won strong reviews, and Cruise and particularly Foxx received excellent notices. Foxx would get an Oscar nomination for Best Supporting Actor for his role, and he might have won had he not also been in the running for Best Actor for the title role in *Ray*, a biopic about singer Ray Charles. *Collateral* earned $100 million at home and another $117 million overseas. Neither *Anchorman* nor *Collateral* was enough to turn DreamWorks around after the battering it had taken for a string of flops; but coming after *Shrek 2*, they improved the outlook for the summer of 2004.

DreamWorks was hot again, at least for the moment, and the troika seized the advantage. In July the studio filed its intent to make an initial public offering (IPO) for DreamWorks Animation SKG. According to the prospectus released that fall, it estimated netting about $624.7 million from the sale of stock. Of that, $269.7 million would be used for "general corporate purposes," including film acquisitions and joint ventures, while some $355 million would be used to pay off outstanding debts from DreamWorks that DreamWorks Animation assumed as a result of the separation. DreamWorks Animation made it clear it was in the computer-generated (CG) film business: "The average domestic box office performance of our CG animated films has been significantly higher than that of our hand-drawn, two-dimensional feature films. We do not have any hand-drawn, two-dimensional films currently in production and do not intend to produce any such films."

More interesting was the glimpse into the management of the new company. Jeffrey Katzenberg would be chief executive officer and a director, and David Geffen and Paul Allen would be directors. But where was Steven Spielberg? The troika received equal shares (8,053,375) of stock as part of the separation, since each had contributed the same amount in setting up DreamWorks. But Geffen and Katzenberg were given Class B stock, each share carrying fifteen votes, while Spielberg took his in Class A stock (what was being sold to the public), where each share had one vote. After the IPO, when various shares were shifted among the principals, Katzenberg and Geffen together could make decisions for the company regardless of what the rest of the stockholders felt. (Paul Allen would also have one share of a separate Class C stock, which would give him the right to appoint a director to the company quite apart from ordinary voting.) This was intended, said the prospectus, to "make us a less attractive takeover target." According to *Business Week Online*, Spielberg decided to decline an official role in the company for fear he would have to reveal his compensation for directing films at DreamWorks. For his part, Katzenberg's commitment of 10 percent of his time to the remaining DreamWorks operation had to be disclosed to prospective investors lest they assume he would devote all his energies to the animation company.

For those able to read the entrails, the prospectus was filled with information not only about the stock offering but about the parent company as well. DreamWorks Animation was estimated to be 20 percent of what was still left of DreamWorks, which meant that the initial valuation of DreamWorks Animation shares would also give the industry some sense of what the remainder of the studio was worth. Likewise, the prospectus noted there would be additional sales of stock to raise sufficient money to allow Paul Allen to recoup his investment.

The release of *Shark Tale* in early October (after showings at the Venice and Toronto film festivals) kept the pot boiling. It was about the partnership of convenience between Oscar (voice of Will Smith), a small fish looking not to be eaten, and Lenny (Jack Black), a mobster shark who is a secret vegetarian. The shark who runs everything—and is Lenny's father—is Don Lino (Robert DeNiro), leading to all sorts of gangster/shark jokes. Indeed, two cast members of the mob TV series *The Sopranos*—Michael Imperioli and Vincent Pastore—also turned up as part of the underwater mob. Some observers found the stereotyping in questionable taste, particularly in an animated family film, but you couldn't tell that to audiences. *Shark Tale* opened with $47 million on opening weekend and finally grossed more than $160 million just in the United States. With *Shrek 2* due out on DVD, it was not surprising that demand for DreamWorks Animation stock was sky high. The IPO share price was expected to be around $23 per share, but because of demand it opened at $28. By the end of the year it was at $40.

Katzenberg would have a studio of his own at last.

13

Merge Ahead

WITH ITS ANIMATION UNIT successfully spun off, what remained of DreamWorks now began its final year as an independent company. All that was left now was the skeletal remains of the television unit, still producing a handful of series, and the live-action feature film division. Although public denials about plans to sell the company continued, DreamWorks did not appear to be a company looking toward the distant future. (The false front was maintained regardless. A letter accompanying the studio's 2005 press preview kit, outlining the year's releases, declared, "This past October, DreamWorks celebrated its 10th anniversary. Now we're looking ahead to a new slate of films as we embark on the next 10 years.")

Already some staff were heading for the exits. Michael DeLuca had left as head of production in 2004 and was replaced by Adam Goodman, who had been with DreamWorks from the beginning and started out as an assistant to Spielberg. Spielberg needed a loyalist in the role since Walter Parkes and Laurie MacDonald were getting out as well. They weren't going very far: they would concentrate on producing their own films to be released by DreamWorks, rather than go through the motions of finding films other than their own to release. Of the eight films on the studio's 2005 schedule, three had Parkes listed as producer and Mac-Donald as producer or executive producer. Of the remaining five, two were from DreamWorks Animation. By May it was official: Parkes and MacDonald set up their own company, Parkes-MacDonald Productions. They would produce two to four films a year, primarily—but not exclusively—for DreamWorks.

In a formal statement announcing the move, Parkes said, "It's no secret that we have wanted to refocus our energies toward producing for some time, but three conditions had to be met before we felt comfortable with the formal shift. First, we wanted the company to be in strong financial shape, which is certainly true after a strong year in 2004 and the splitting off of animation. Second, we wanted there to be a strong slate of films, which we feel is the case for 2005 and 2006. And finally, and perhaps most importantly, we wanted to feel secure about who would be picking up the reins of the day-to-day running of the studio."

It would be months before DreamWorks would admit it was for sale, even as talks went on quietly behind the scenes. There would be considerable bad news along the way. *The Ring Two* was a cheesy attempt to cash in on the surprise success of the first film, but interest in the "J-horror" fad had already passed. Interestingly, while star Naomi Watts returned for the sequel, director Gore Verbinski proved to be unavailable. When another director didn't pan out, Dream-Works brought in Japanese director Hideo Nakata to make his American debut. Nakata had not only directed the original *Ringu* but had also directed the sequel in Japan. *The Ring Two* owed nothing to that sequel, but the fact that Nakata had done the original films gave *The Ring Two* some pre-release cachet. "This was the man who literally created the mythology we are trying to explore," said Parkes, who produced with MacDonald. He was overstating the case, as the Japanese films were in fact based on a series of novels by Japanese horror writer Koji Suzuki.

In the end, it didn't matter. Although the film opened strong in March 2005 with $35 million the opening weekend, it topped out at just under $76 million, compared to $128 million for *The Ring*. Overseas grosses were also down: $66.8 million for the sequel compared to $100.6 million for the original.

Fortunately DreamWorks had its big gun set to launch the summer season, the first release from the newly public DreamWorks Animation, *Madagascar*. To introduce it the studio set up special screenings with sample footage not only for the press but for anyone who was involved in cross-promotion efforts. Focusing on the adventures of four animals from the Central Park Zoo who end up in Africa—voiced by Ben Stiller, Jada Pinkett Smith, David Schwimmer, and Chris Rock—it was a thoroughly entertaining cartoon, nearly stolen by a group of penguin conspirators (one of whom was voiced by one of the film's directors, Tom Mc-Grath) and the king of the lemurs (a hilarious turn by Sacha Baron Cohen). Reviews were lukewarm, but business was good. That was the problem: business wasn't great. For DreamWorks Animation investors who had watched their stock value increase, they now had to face the reality that there are no guarantees in the entertainment business, and that not every release from the new animation studio would perform like *Shrek 2*. The movie grossed $100 million in nine days, but the stock fell to $28, a loss of 27 percent in just one month. (It had previously gone as high as $42.60 per share.) Wall Street had expected a megahit instead of an ordinary one, particularly since animation executives were reporting that *Madagascar* had done better with test audiences than the original *Shrek*.

"When you talk up a film the way they did, you'd better deliver," said financial analyst Richard Greenfield of Fulcrum Global Partners LLC.

It wasn't just the fact that *Madagascar*—which eventually earned a total worldwide gross of $518 million, nearly $200 million of it in the United States—didn't immediately seem like a smash. There was the further problem that *Shrek 2* had underperformed on DVD. The original *Shrek* had sold 49 million DVDs, and given the huge success of *Shrek 2* it did not seem out of line to project 55 million units of the sequel flying off the shelves. They didn't. In what came to be regarded as one of the first signs of an industrywide trend, the sales of *Shrek 2* seemed to indicate that the DVD market had matured much more rapidly than anyone expected. DVD players were now standard electronic equipment in many homes, and people didn't feel the need to rush out and buy a bunch of DVDs in order to have something to play. By June *Shrek 2* had sold an impressive 35 million units, but that was impressive only if you didn't compare it to *Shrek* or to the earlier projections. DreamWorks was far from the only studio discovering that consumers would not buy everything on DVD, including hit films. Its chief rival in computer animation, Pixar, had had a remarkable run, with *The Incredibles* its sixth consecutive hit film without a flop. Yet Pixar had to lower its earnings prediction for the second quarter of 2005 because it was getting many more returns on the DVD release of *The Incredibles* than it had expected. When this failure to perform to expectations repeated with the DVD release of *Shark Tale*, DreamWorks Animation shares dropped below their original $28 asking price.

The honeymoon with Wall Street was over. DreamWorks Animation found itself the subject of several shareholder lawsuits, claiming that false and misleading statements had been made about the company's prospects. Those lawsuits will likely amount to nothing, but it was a headache the company didn't need. Katzenberg tried to put the best face on it, promising an investigation to see why the market-place was responding as it did and what could be done about it. "I think it would be imprudent to come to a conclusion about this yet," he said.

In many ways, July 2005 marked the beginning of the end for DreamWorks. With Katzenberg occupied with Dream-Works Animation and Spielberg off on his second film for the year (*Munich*, which would be released in December), Hollywood was surprised to learn that it would be the third member of the troika who emerged as the person running the studio. At least David Geffen became its spokesperson. Day-to-day operations remained in the hands of Adam Goodman and chief operating officer Rick Sands, who had come from Miramax. If there was a new DreamWorks phi-losophy, it seemed as diffuse as the old. It would continue to handle quirky little films like *The Prize Winner of Defiance, Ohio* (Julianne Moore as a 1950s housewife and mother who helps support her large family by entering contests), but it was now in business with filmmaker Michael Bay, a director known for blockbuster films like *Bad Boys*, *The Rock*, *Armageddon*, and *Pearl Harbor*. Bay had two films set up at DreamWorks. One was *Transform-ers*, an action film inspired by a line of 1980s toys and a TV cartoon series. The other was the studio's bid for a traditional summer smash: *The Island*. Said Sands, "We still want to make important movies, but I do believe the palette is broadening."

Although busy elsewhere, Katzenberg and Spielberg kept their hands in. Bay reported that Spielberg contacted him about directing *The Island*, and offered him advice during the shoot: "It's pretty funny—he was watching all my dailies. *Spielberg* watching your dailies!"

With Spielberg's *War of the Worlds* doing well (Dream-Works had a piece of the action for the Paramount release) and *The Island* about to open, things looked bright. It turned out to be a perfect time to begin talks with Universal Studios about a merger or buyout. When the story became public, DreamWorks immediately denied it—but then it denied the denial, saying the truth was that the company didn't comment on such stories. Speculation was that a Securities and Exchange Commission investigation into DreamWorks Animation had everyone on edge. While the two companies were now separate, there was so much overlap among the principals—not to mention the fact that DreamWorks was the distributor for DreamWorks Animation—that it was deemed prudent for everyone involved to say nothing.

In spite of denials, talks were indeed proceeding, and the key question for the parties was figuring out how much DreamWorks was worth. Its entire library of some sixty movies included a few major hits, but many of them were co-productions with other studios. Would a deal also include the services of Spielberg? It became clear that anyone acquiring DreamWorks would also be acquiring Spielberg loyalists Goodman, Parkes, and MacDonald. In August DreamWorks announced it had extended Goodman's contract for four years to 2009, and the deal with Parkes-MacDonald Productions through 2008. It was Geffen who praised Goodman in the official announcement: "Adam Goodman has been an integral part of our production team since the inception of the studio and, over the past year and a half, he has more than proven his capability to lead that team."

Universal too declined comment about talks, but it was not hard to see what the attraction was, given that Spielberg and the DreamWorks offices were already located in Universal City, and that UIP (jointly owned by Universal and Paramount and about to break up) handled DreamWorks releases overseas. Spielberg, Katzenberg, and Geffen all had good relations with top Universal executives, and the two studios were partners on the comedy hit *Meet the Parents*. Universal had also been handling all of DreamWorks's releases on DVD. There were already so many ties between the two that folding DreamWorks into Universal's operations would be a lot smoother than being absorbed by any other studio.

The release of *The Island*, then, could not have come at a worse time. With a budget estimated to be $130 million, this was a film that needed to be a smash hit, or at least enough of a success worldwide to warrant the investment. Instead it turned out to be one of the biggest—and most embarrassing—flops of 2005. It opened to scathing reviews and only $12 million at the box office. With hindsight there were plenty of reasons offered for its failure. Some believed the timing was wrong, with *Wedding Crashers* and *Charlie and the Chocolate Factory* having just opened and generating a good deal of word of mouth. There was some thought about delaying the film until later in the year, but DreamWorks was locked into the summer release schedule because of later foreign openings. "The biggest mistake this company made was we made a date, not a movie," said publicity chief Terry Press, being unusually frank.

Some blamed the rushed production schedule, which left the studio without a finished print to show until only two weeks before the opening. Others pointed to the confusing marketing campaign. The story was an action-thriller involving clones who discover they have been created to provide spare parts for their originals; DreamWorks couldn't decide whether to promote it as an action film or a science-fiction adventure. A reported 650 poster ideas and 75 proposed ads were generated in the search for a handle on the film, making it clear that no one was quite sure what to do with it. Some at the studio even blamed the stars for not being big enough to open the film, but then it wasn't Ewan McGregor or Scarlett Johansson who forced themselves onto the project. (Ironically the film, which would earn around $36 million domestically, did much better with a retooled marketing campaign overseas, racking up $125 million. It was still considered a flop, but it was a little less humiliating.)

The fallout was more than just having to write off another embarrassing failure and then wait around through the rest of the summer since there would be no more DreamWorks releases until after Labor Day. Universal, which had been acquired by General Electric and merged with the NBC television network, was going through a process of financial self-scrutiny and belt-tightening. *The Island* had become the season's symbol of out-of-control spending with nothing to show for it. Even if the executives cared to argue that they got what they paid for, it was hardly an advertisement for cost-effective film production. It led some to wonder if DreamWorks was being overvalued, particularly in GE's executive offices. DreamWorks and Universal had agreed to a two-month period in which neither side would speak publicly about a potential merger. During that time DreamWorks would deal exclusively with Universal and not look for other suitors. In September the negotiations were abruptly called off.

"We pursued it for quite some time, we were unable to come to terms, and we're no longer in discussions with them," said Geffen. The asking price was apparently the sticking point, but there was also speculation that Spielberg was refusing to agree to be tied down by any deal. From Universal's perspective, a promise that they *might* get one or more Spielberg movies as part of the deal was worthless. Of course Geffen was known as the dealmaker of the troika, and he was known for playing hardball. DreamWorks's deal with UIP gave it the right to walk away when Universal and Paramount dissolved their joint foreign distribution company, as they had announced they would be doing, and that gave DreamWorks additional leverage with Universal. It could forge a new overseas deal with a different company and cut out Universal altogether.

Through the fall of 2005 speculation persisted as to whether another suitor would emerge or Universal and DreamWorks would go back to the table. Eventually they reopened negotiations, but in early December the board of directors of Viacom, owners of Paramount, gave the go-ahead for the studio to pursue its own merger talks with DreamWorks. Now under pressure from a competitor, why couldn't Universal lock up the deal? The stumbling blocks continued to be price—DreamWorks was valuing itself at $1 billion and asking for that plus the assumption of debt—and a firm commitment from Spielberg as part of the acquisition. From the initial announcement to the bitter end, Spielberg had always been the company's greatest asset and bargaining chip, and he had made successful films at both studios. In the end, though, Spielberg was about the movies he wanted on his schedule, and not those he was obligated to do.

For its part, Paramount had every reason to make a deal. Beyond needing product overseas given the pending dissolution of UIP (the same situation that was motivating Universal), there had just been an executive upheaval at the studio. Brad Grey had been put in charge to turn Paramount around after several lackluster years. He had brought in Gail Berman, fresh from several years running the FOX network, but it would still be a multiyear process to crank up Paramount's production schedule. DreamWorks's slate of eight or so films a year would be a big help in that regard. Paramount had hesitated because Viacom was in the midst of a split in which their radio and television elements (CBS and Infinity Broadcasting) would be spun off into a separate company.

Once Paramount had Viacom's approval, things moved quickly. DreamWorks and Universal had been close to a deal before Thanksgiving, but a balky General Electric insisted on additional financial figures from DreamWorks, apparently in hopes of lowering the price (a reported $1.4 billion including the assumption of debt). Universal then asked DreamWorks to lower the price by about $200 million. After the flop of *The Island*, DreamWorks had stumbled through the fall with *Just Like Heaven*, a romantic comedy with Reese Witherspoon as a ghost, and *Dreamer*, a horse story with Kurt Russell and Dakota Fanning. Those three films alone bled $60 million in red ink, and GE wanted a price adjustment for the sale.

According to someone close to the negotiations, this was a mistake and may have cost Universal the prize: "You can't believe how upset that made David. For him it was a matter of honor. He thought he had a deal." Reportedly only hours away from announcing an agreement, the move by General Electric made DreamWorks ripe for an offer from another suitor. When Paramount offered more than Universal ($1.6 billion), Geffen was ready to move ahead, but he and Katzenberg still needed Spielberg's okay. Besides being the key partner, he had his long-standing relationship with Universal, where he had gotten his first break more than three decades earlier. Spielberg met with Paramount's Grey and Viacom CEO Tom Freston and apparently got whatever assurances he needed. It was no doubt a plus that a merger with Paramount would create an association with the Nickelodeon cable channel—a mostly animated channel geared to kids—which was potentially lucrative for DreamWorks Animation. Although the animation unit was not part of the deal, it had a long-term commitment to release its animated films through DreamWorks.

Trying to make the numbers work on their end, Paramount immediately began exploring the possibility of selling off the DreamWorks library while retaining the right to distribute the films. This would produce a lot of cash up front to take the sting out of the deal, and allow Paramount to continue to collect a distribution fee for those films in the future. Paramount also lined up private investors to share the burden of the DreamWorks acquisition. What it had come down to was that General Electric considered this a business proposition and Viacom looked at it as a Hollywood deal. If DreamWorks was about anything, it was the Hollywood deal. "The value for Paramount was irrefutable," said Viacom's Freston, "and we turned everything upside down to get the deal done."

"I was saddened that after long negotiations and many compromises we were unable to come to terms with Universal's parent company, GE," said Spielberg in a prepared statement. It was hard to tell if he was thumbing his nose at them or trying to keep the door open at Universal by shifting the blame for the collapsed deal to GE. Spielberg's contract with Paramount was for only three years, but as he had had dealings with the studio before—including the recent *War of the Worlds*—apparently it wasn't a stumbling block for Spielberg and was a positive attraction for Paramount. Said one Viacom executive, "There are only three real brand names in the movie business—Spielberg, Pixar, and Miramax—and Spielberg is number one."

Paramount eased its costs in early 2006 when it made a complex deal with Soros Strategic Partners and Dune Entertainment to sell off the DreamWorks film library for $900 million. What made it complex was that Viacom/Paramount retained some ownership interests including music, sequel, and merchandising rights, as well as a minority interest in the entity actually owning the films. In addition, it would have the exclusive right to distribute the films for five years. After that, if one side hadn't bought out the other side—in other words, if Paramount didn't either buy back or sell off its interests—the distribution agreement would automatically renew. In many ways it was a long-term loan secured by the film library. The "interest" would consist of the share of revenues going to Soros/Dune and the promise of "market value" for the library should DreamWorks choose to reacquire the library in the future. What it seemed to accomplish in the near term was to reduce Paramount's net payout for acquiring DreamWorks to somewhere in the neighborhood of $600 million, making the company seem like a bargain.

As the dust settled, it was clear that an era had come to a close. Although DreamWorks Animation would continue, and the DreamWorks logo would survive—at least in the near term—on the films it produced and released through Paramount, it was time for everyone to wake up to the reality of business in Hollywood in the twenty-first century. There would be no room for any more dreaming.

Epilogue:
Why Did DreamWorks Fail?

ANY DISCUSSION of why DreamWorks failed must begin by asking what is meant by "failure." By several standards, DreamWorks must be considered a successful enterprise.

The troika—Spielberg, Katzenberg, and Geffen—clearly got what they wanted out of it. Spielberg enhanced his already towering position as a Hollywood power broker without having to sacrifice any of what is clearly his primary professional interest and priority, making movies. He remained free to work on films at other studios, though he required most of them to be turned into co-productions with DreamWorks. Along the way he had several hit films, including *Saving Private Ryan*, which stands with *E.T.* and *Schindler's List* at the pinnacle of his extraordinarily successful career.

Katzenberg had the most to lose by starting up Dream-Works. Where Spielberg and Geffen essentially wrote checks for their share of the initial investment, Katzenberg had to mortgage his house. He also entered DreamWorks as someone with a reputation as a tenacious and successful film executive—who had always worked for other people. Katzenberg came through the process not only financially whole but in a far better position than he was in 1994 (winning his lawsuit against Disney for a share of the profits undoubtedly helped). As chief executive officer of Dream-Works Animation, his was the first studio to successfully challenge Disney—both at the box office and in acclaim from critics and within the industry—in the realm of feature animated films.

Geffen, who came into DreamWorks with enough wealth to last several lifetimes, clearly didn't wish to be a day-to-day executive in the entertainment industry for a third go-round, and he wasn't. He rarely showed up at the DreamWorks offices, even as he stayed in touch with Katzenberg and Spielberg, and he spent his time with the investments, philanthropy, and political fund-raising that were clearly his priorities. His involvement with Dream-Works allowed him to keep a hand in the industry and to step in with advice or with the savvy deal-making skills that his partners appreciated. The company was so trivial in terms of his own personal finances that some reports suggested he planned to donate any DreamWorks profits he might realize to charity.

One is hard-pressed to argue that any of the three founders "failed" as a result of his involvement with Dream-Works. Likewise, the other private investors, particularly Paul Allen, appeared to be satisfied with their end of the deal. According to Geffen, Allen had already cashed out his initial investment on the stock offering for DreamWorks Animation. Allen's share of the Paramount sale, according to Geffen, was "profit for him."

When one looks at what DreamWorks turned out, it includes three movies that were nominated for the Best Picture Oscar, of which two of them (*American Beauty* and *Gladiator*) won. The studio produced the first animated feature to win the new Oscar in that category. It also produced the single most successful animated feature—in terms of worldwide box office—in history (*Shrek 2*). This too cannot be easily dismissed as failure.

Since the Golden Age of Hollywood there have been many attempts to start new studios or production entities, Orion Pictures, DeLaurentiis Entertainment Group, Vestron, and CarolCo Pictures among them. Some had a few big hits, but all these companies were eventually bought out or went under. DreamWorks was supposed to be different. After all, it was headed by three of the most successful men in the entertainment business, with Steven Spielberg the director behind some of the most popular movies made since the mid-1970s. These were not some anonymous suits who got lucky with a fluke hit like *Dirty Dancing* or *Rambo*. They had a proven track record and, what's more, a vision of what the studio of the twenty-first century ought to be. It would be a place with state-of-the-art technology, where producers and directors—and even screenwriters—were regarded as artistic and financial partners in the process. There would be no hierarchy; no one would even have a title. All would be equal and able to do their best work, and synergy would flow across film, television, music, and interactive games.

DreamWorks failed because it could not live up to the dream that its founders defined for it. Bit by bit they scaled it back. That modern studio facility would not be built—except for the animators in Glendale. The interactive effort had talented people at the ground level, and the music arm did too. No one at the top, though, felt either effort was a priority, and both were eventually sold off after lackluster returns.

A greater effort was made on the television side, and if Disney had not bought ABC, perhaps the ABC/DreamWorks deal would have led to great success. As it was, ABC ran the only unqualified series success DreamWorks had, *Spin City*. Of three cable miniseries, two were successful—*Taken* on the Sci-Fi Channel and *Band of Brothers* on HBO—while the partnership with NBC enjoyed some success thanks to *Las Vegas*. Yet television too was never a major priority for DreamWorks, as Katzenberg's cold feet over the Maury Povich / Connie Chung show demonstrated. When it grew too risky, the answer was no.

The DreamWorks founders had a vision of creating their own reality and not having to answer to anyone else. In a 2000 interview, David Geffen remarked, "We started DreamWorks because it allows us to do what we do in an atmosphere where we are in charge of it. We're not frustrated by having to deal with other people and their agendas and their priorities and their tastes. We're dealing with our own."

Brave words, but also empty ones. The basic economic rules governing any business enterprise had not been repealed, and DreamWorks had to generate big revenues to cover its costs and loans as well as to justify its very existence. If it was turning out films that could have come from any other studio, what difference was it making? Only four years later Geffen was making excuses: "Our eyes were bigger than our stomachs. We did what we could do. We started a number of things that turned out not to be good ideas. The world has changed a great deal in ten years."

Part of DreamWorks's problem was that the business had indeed consolidated greatly over the decade. When Rupert Murdoch began the FOX network in the 1980s with Barry Diller and Jamie Kellner, it had been considered folly, just as starting a new studio in the nineties was thought to be a near impossibility. But Murdoch had three advantages that DreamWorks lacked. First, in Twentieth Century Fox he had an already successful studio that produced and distributed films, and also produced and distributed television programs. Second, he had a marketplace of numerous independent television stations willing to consider affiliation with a new fourth network, and a growth in cable service that would give his mostly UHF stations the means to compete with the established networks on an equal footing.

Before turning to the third advantage, consider for a moment that DreamWorks already lacked the first two. It can be argued that the studio might never have succeeded in any case, but trying to do several things at once, as opposed to first launching a film production company and then expanding into other areas as it grew successful, doomed it from the start. Fox did not launch its cable channels, like FX and FOX News, for example, until the broadcast network was established. As to the marketplace, the entertainment industry was not conducive to a start-up like DreamWorks. By the late nineties most studios were well established in both production and distribution. Disney could produce a film, put it in theaters around the world, release it on its video label, issue a soundtrack recording on CD, put it on one of its cable channels, and then air it on its ABC television network—and sell much of the ancillary product in its own Disney Stores. When DreamWorks wanted to release a movie outside North America, it was usually dealing with UIP, which took a cut of the box office for its efforts. When DreamWorks released a movie on home video, it was through Universal where, once again, it was at the mercy of a company that had its own product to sell. That's not to say that Universal gave short shrift to

DreamWorks, but it did put DreamWorks at a remove from the process. The upside was that Geffen had negotiated a deal (using Spielberg's continued presence at Universal City as leverage) that worked to DreamWorks's financial advantage, but it still meant that DreamWorks had to deal with the "agendas and priorities and tastes" of people outside the company.

When it came time to renegotiate the home-video deal, Universal had new owners and didn't rush to renew. Dream-Works entered into lengthy talks with Warner Bros. to see if it could get a better distribution deal there, but those negotiations eventually broke down. According to one executive reported to be "close to the situation," it was Warners that decided it wasn't worth it: "DreamWorks is . . . high maintenance. It's not worth it when you have to deal with them every day." DreamWorks ended up back with Universal, on favorable financial terms, yet Warners didn't seem to think it had lost out. According to one report, studio executives felt they didn't need the headache of distributing DreamWorks movies. "There was a moment in time when [Warner] would have given them anything. With vertical integration, nobody needs them. . . . Those days are way over." So DreamWorks tried to do too much too soon, and the marketplace didn't see the studio as providing a new financial opportunity that made people want to go into business with them. It was one thing to attract investors on the strength of the names of the founders. It was another when potential business arrangements fell through because other companies felt they weren't worth the effort.

The third reason FOX succeeded and DreamWorks failed was the nature of the people at the very top. Murdoch had been looking for a toehold in Hollywood for several years, and he was ready and eager when the opportunity to invest in Twentieth Century Fox arose. Barry Diller had been involved in the abortive attempt to launch a fourth network at Paramount in the late seventies. When the two of them got together, you had two people who were raring to show the world that they understood the business better than the naysayers, and willing to gamble and take big risks to show they were right.

Bob Bennett, who worked for John Kluge—whose Metromedia stations would become the cornerstone of the new FOX network—noted that people such as Kluge and Murdoch were like riverboat gamblers, willing to take a chance on various deals where they might lose vast sums because the potential returns made the risk worth it. Once, Bennett was negotiating the purchase of a station for Kluge and trying to lower the sale price from $14 million to $10 million. When Kluge found this out he told Bennett to pay the higher price, because "it really doesn't make any difference." When Kluge sold his stations to Murdoch two years later, the one he had overpaid for at $14 million was bought by Murdoch for $65 million.

No one at DreamWorks was willing to play for those stakes. Paul Allen certainly put up a lot of money, but he had a degree of protection on the back end and was never involved in the day-to-day operations of the company. Spielberg and Geffen made it clear they had little interest in running the studio, with Geffen rarely even on the premises. One can hardly blame Geffen for not wanting to ride herd on DreamWorks Music, having already built up and sold two profitable music labels. It does explain, though, why even the veteran management couldn't make a go of it when the three entrepreneurs couldn't be bothered.

The Playa Vista studio may have been doomed, but it fell apart in the end when the troika was told they'd have to start risking some of their own money on the project because the company couldn't afford it. No riverboat gamblers here. The plug was pulled on the Playa Vista studio just as it would later be pulled on Pop.com.

What it came down to was hunger for success. That explains why DreamWorks Animation currently exists as a publicly traded company and DreamWorks, as an independent producer of live-action films, is now merely a logo owned by Paramount. There is no question that when it came to the animation side, Jeffrey Katzenberg was hungry. He wanted the financial success he felt was his due, but he also wanted the authority he believed he had earned after years of working for other people. He had something to prove, and he took big risks. Some, like *Shrek*, paid off spectacularly. Some, like *Sinbad* and *Road to El Dorado*, flopped. Katzenberg learned, adapted, and stayed focused. When it became clear in 2005 that Katzenberg was at a disadvantage as an inexperienced CEO of a publicly traded company— even as he and Geffen retained most of the real power—he did the shrewd thing. In December he persuaded Lewis Coleman, a former vice chairman and chief financial officer of Bank of America, to move off the board of directors of DreamWorks Animation and take on the newly created job of president. Coleman reports to Katzenberg, as other parts of the company now report to Coleman. This was seen as a gesture reassuring Wall Street that the inmates were not running the asylum, and that Katzenberg was prepared to do what was necessary to see that the company was stable and financially secure. More important, he could speak the language investors understood, rather than the glitter and hype that was the common coinage in Hollywood.

"Lew will take on a lot of very important day-to-day responsibilities of running a public company and allow me to focus more of my time on partnerships, marketing of our movies and the movies themselves," said Katzenberg. He was acknowledging his limitations, playing to his strengths, and delegating those responsibilities he felt others could handle better. It was the sort of leadership rarely seen at DreamWorks.

Given the nature of the movie business today, where essentially six companies—Time-Warner, General Electric, Walt Disney, Sony, Viacom, and NewsCorp.—control most of the film production in Hollywood, it seems likely, indeed inevitable, that DreamWorks Animation will eventually become part of a larger enterprise. At the time DreamWorks was closing the deal with Paramount, its more successful rival in animation, Pixar, announced it was merging with Disney. When the day comes that DreamWorks Animation decides to forgo its independence, it will be on terms that Katzenberg and—to the extent that he cares—Geffen decide is acceptable. It will not be because running a studio has become a chore and a distraction. DreamWorks Animation succeeded because Katzenberg made its success his priority.

On the live-action side, Steven Spielberg clearly had little interest in being a movie mogul. It was fine to hold press conferences or to drop into the film offices or phone directors with advice, but DreamWorks was not about to replace his own moviemaking career. During the eleven years of Dream-Works, Spielberg directed nine pictures, or almost one per year. Of those nine, five were for other studios, and *Saving Private Ryan* became a DreamWorks release in the United States only by the flip of a coin. This was not a man who was putting his best efforts into making the studio work. But since DreamWorks was privately held, as long as his choices were okay with his partners, it was no one else's business. (By contrast, when DreamWorks Animation went public,

Katzenberg had to quantify and limit the amount of time he would devote to DreamWorks—as opposed to Animation—business.)

Spielberg's role was supposed to be acceptable because he put William Parkes and Laurie MacDonald at the head of live-action film production. But they had huge conflicts of interest since they continued as producers, including producing films at other studios. Spielberg gave them his full backing right up to the end, when their production deal with DreamWorks was extended before the studio was sold. He was proud of their place at DreamWorks: "If they weren't as good as they are and as proactive as they are and as ambitious as they are, I really couldn't have been a co-studio head and a director."

This may have been reassuring to Spielberg, but it made some filmmakers reluctant to go to DreamWorks. If they got their deal set up there, Parkes and MacDonald might come attached as producers, meaning both creative and financial interference. Said one producer at the time, "Walter is in a giant, giant conflict-of-interest position right now. He's running the studio and sort of cherry-picking the best projects and attaching himself as a producer and getting paid as a producer." Neither Spielberg nor Parkes and MacDonald could be said to unambiguously have the best interests of DreamWorks as their primary concern. That doesn't mean they necessarily did anything unethical, since the conflict was obviously well known to everyone, but it did serve to undercut DreamWorks at a time when it should have been fighting for every last advantage.

Spielberg's name was clearly a tremendous asset to DreamWorks, and if it was determined that keeping him out there making movies was the best use of his time, so be it. But DreamWorks needed someone at the top who would nurture and develop and go to bat for film production the way Katzenberg did for animation. However talented and successful they are as producers, Parkes and MacDonald were clearly not the people for the job since they were unwilling to give up their own shingle. In effect they were in direct competition with the filmmakers who were pitching films to their studio. Here was a company that had promised to be different, but it was supposed to be empowering filmmakers, not undercutting them.

In spite of some unquestioned successes, the live-action film division largely bought into the industry culture and failed to create a distinctive niche for itself because no one in charge seemed to be interested in doing that. While it would be nice to point to DreamWorks's hits as proof that the studio was on the cutting edge, it was instead perceived by filmmakers as Parkes and MacDonald looking out for themselves.

In the end, DreamWorks was built on a premise that it could change the way things were done in Hollywood because, after all, its principals were Steven Spielberg, Jeffrey Katzenberg, and David Geffen. Many people who should have known better went along with the dream because they too believed these guys were special. When it came time to wake up, it turned out that nothing had changed. The way the business was being run would continue to apply to everyone.

Even the Dream Team.

As noted at the beginning of the book, this history of DreamWorks was written without its cooperation. But in March 2006 the author secured a tantalizingly brief moment with Jeffrey Katzenberg that perhaps serves as a coda to the story.

Katzenberg was on a whirlwind eight-city tour promoting the year's animation releases. The gathering in Boston was shown a seven-minute clip from *Flushed Away*, a collaboration between Nick Parks (who had just won an Oscar for *Wallace and Gromit: Curse of the Were-Rabbit*, a DreamWorks release) and DreamWorks Animation. It would be Parks's first serious foray into computer animation. The film, scheduled for November 2006 release, was still in production.

Also on hand were actress Wanda Sykes and co-director Tim Johnson from *Over the Hedge*, the studio's early summer release. Sykes and Johnson were doing interviews, with Katzenberg briefly available. Then the press and local promotional partners were invited to a breakfast at the AMC Boston Common Theaters (the buffet included two kinds of imported bottled waters) to see the *Flushed Away* clip and a nearly complete print of *Over the Hedge*. A nervous Johnson noted that some 10 percent of the film was incomplete (about fifty or sixty shots), which made him feel like he was standing naked in front of the audience. "If you see anything in the movie that's not done, it's not done," said Johnson, in what would become a running joke in his remarks. Studios sometimes must show unfinished versions of films to journalists with long lead times, or because special effects were not yet finished by the time of a previously scheduled junket. It takes supreme confidence to showcase an unfinished film to the press, knowing that opinions will be formed based on a version the public will never see.

Katzenberg appeared briefly. He was dressed in what might almost be considered his uniform: plain slacks, a white T-shirt, and a blue pullover sweater. He might be the CEO of one of the remaining independents in Hollywood, but he was no suit.

He showed up shortly before the 11 a.m. screening to take photos with Johnson and Sykes for the local press, and then introduce the films and the talent. "This last year 2005 was a very exciting year for our company," he said, referring to DreamWorks but meaning DreamWorks Animation. He mentioned the Oscar for *Wallace and Gromit* and the financial success of *Madagascar*, but not the sale of DreamWorks or the shaky state of the DVD market. A short and unassuming man, youthful in appearance at age fifty-five in spite of his baldness, Katzenberg seemed relaxed, comfortable with his success and his place in the world.

Perhaps more important, he showed himself a man who now knows that he doesn't know everything, and that admitting that he doesn't know everything is fine. Early on at DreamWorks he had spoken in sweeping and absolute tones. *Prince of Egypt* would be a landmark film. *Spirit: Stallion of the Cimarron* would lead to a new fusion of traditional and computer animation. The failure of *Sinbad: Legend of the Seven Seas* was proof that traditional animation was dead. Indeed, the prospectus for DreamWorks Animation made it clear that the new public company had no intention of turning the clock back by ever returning to hand-drawn animation.

But the Academy Award nominations for Best Animated Feature of 2005 had gone to three films that were all old-fashioned in technique, using computers on a limited basis if at all: the stop-motion *Wallace and Gromit* and *Tim Burton's Corpse Bride*, and the hand-drawn *Howl's Movie Castle* from Japan's Hayao Miyazaki. None of the year's new CGI films—*Robots*, *Chicken Little*, *Valiant*, *Hoodwinked*, or DreamWorks's own *Madagascar*—made the cut. Katzenberg now was entertaining second thoughts and publicly reconsidering his declaration that computer animation was the only way to go. In interviews he said that traditional or 2D (two-dimensional) animation remained a viable format, requiring the right script to make it work. If someone came up with the right script, he explained, there could still be an audience for a traditionally animated film.

In the crowded lobby of the Boston Common Theater, Katzenberg was asked if that meant he had reconsidered his early dismissal of hand-drawn animation in favor of doing it all by computer. Was DreamWorks really committed to its early decision to focus strictly on computer animation?

Katzenberg smiled at the question, answering, "Never say, 'Never again.'"

For all practical purposes, the DreamWorks story is over. But the story of DreamWorks Animation may be just beginning.

Notes

Prologue: Happy Anniversary

page

5 "[S]ince any successful business is . . . for your unflagging loyalty and commitment." DreamWorks advertisement, *Daily Variety*, Gotham Edition, October 15, 2004, pp. 3–6.

5 The fourth page was . . . keeping at DreamWorks. Ibid.

1: Dramatis Personae

10 According to his biographer . . . sometimes been reported. Joseph McBride, *Steven Spielberg: A Biography* (New York, 1997), pp. 35–36.

12–13 As Spielberg biographer . . . paying homage to his own movies." Ibid., p. 305.

13 "It says nothing of consequence . . . hooked on the crap of his childhood." Mason Wiley and Damien Bona, *Inside Oscar* (New York, 1988), p. 600.

15 According to Geffen's biographer . . . treated Geffen shabbily. Tom King, *The Operator* (New York, 2000), pp. 41–43.

17 "That was the quickest ride . . . younger version of himself in Katzenberg. Ibid., p. 254.

18 "You are going to become a fanatic . . . build your collection." Ibid., p. 358.

19 "It's not a bummer, you know? It's nothing." Ibid., p. 499.

20 Over several days, whatever problems . . . a large check made out to Nimoy. Judith and Garfield Reeves-Stevens, *Star Trek: Phase II—The Lost Series* (New York, 1997), p. 77.

20 He was so good . . . the "Golden Retriever." King, *Operator*, p. 383.

21 Katzenberg thrived . . . a project was Madonna. John Taylor, *Storming the Magic Kingdom* (New York, 1987), pp. 241–242.

22 "Take the money and stay . . . It'll all work out." King, *Operator*, p. 508.

2: Present at the Creation

23 "Jeffrey was a believer . . . felt the loss. Anita M. Busch, "Roth Rattles Nerves at Neuro Disney," *Variety*, August 29, 1994, pp. 1, 54.

23 *Variety*, noting . . . yet to make a major move himself." Adam Sandler, "Inside Moves: Mega-Exex on the Loose," *Variety*, August 29, 1994, p. 4.

24 He spent the day . . . "table-hopping in the executive dining room." John Brodie, "Who's Minding the Store," *Variety*, October 3, 1994, p. 1.

24 His friend Geffen . . . You can do it." King, *Operator* (New York, 2000), p. 518.

27 It was Katzenberg . . . Certainly it's my Dream Team." Ibid., p. 532.

27 Arnold Rifkin . . . provide cash flow and sustain overhead." John Brodie, "Troika Tweaks MCA," *Variety*, October 17, 1994, pp. 1, 178.

27–28 *Variety* editor-in-chief Peter Bart . . . all the autonomy you could ever want?" Peter Bart, "Weaving the Dream," *Variety*, October 31, 1994, pp. 4, 103.

29 *Variety's* Peter Bart noted . . . they *are* the establishment." Peter Bart, "The Best Laid Dreams," *Variety*, January 30, 1995, p. 8.

29 Paul Allen . . . wanted to be in the entertainment business." Mark Stahlman, "The Lure of Silliwood Strikes Again," *Computer Reseller News*, March 27, 1995, p. 14.

29 "The potential for combining the incredible stories . . . Gates enthused. Greg Spring, "DreamWorks Attracts Two Big Names," *Los Angeles Business Journal*, March 27, 1995, p. 5.

30 Said one potential lender . . . this deal is almost a must." Daniel Dunaief, "Chemical Wins Starring Role in $1B Loan to Spiel-

berg & Co.'s Multimedia Venture," *American Banker*, March 31, 1995, p. 1.

30 In March the DreamWorks team . . . multimedia company of the new millennium." Richard Corliss, "Hey, Let's Put on a Show!" *Time*, March 27, 1995, p. 54.

31 "I have not just figuratively bet the ranch . . . the success of this company." Ibid.

31 "We could have built this up . . . before I fall asleep at night." Ibid.

3: A Room of One's Own

34 "I'm pleased as hell . . . to get a project like this." Ted Johnson, "Troika Stakes Out Turf," *Variety*, December 18, 1995, p. 20.

35 Indeed . . . this would be the "prototype community of the future." Ibid.

35 "Most of the other studios . . . That's what we wanted." James Sterngold, "Vast New DreamWorks Film Lot," *New York Times*, December 14, 1995, p. C11.

36 "After the '94 earthquake in LA . . . I think nobody even knew." Interview with Ruth Galanter, July 22, 2005.

37 Galanter recalled, "We could point to places . . . we've got to get something for it," she told them. Ibid.

37–38 The *Los Angeles Business Journal* . . . the final hurdle in the plan's approval." Brad Berton and Greg Spring, "DreamWorks Finds a Home," *Los Angeles Business Journal*, December 4, 1995, p. 1.

38 "Initially they tried to paint us . . . protests at their events," he said. Interview with Bruce Robertson, July 18, 2005.

38 Commenting on the numerous wildlife . . . of the environmental claims. Quoted on KCAL-TV newscast, January 8, 1996.

39 "It was particularly galling . . . urban Los Angeles." Galanter interview.

39 Spielberg said the tanks were "something all directors are crying for." Rex Weiner and Katherine Stalter, "Studio Dream at Work," *Variety*, July 1, 1996, p. 33.

40 Steve McDonald . . . put this thing together." Brad Berton, "DreamWorks Stuck in Limbo," *Los Angeles Business Journal*, October 14, 1996, p. 1.

40 Commenting on all the . . . by the time it gets its own studio." Jason Vest, "No Dream for Them," *U.S. News and World Report*, November 4, 1996, p. 54.

41 "We're not waiting any longer . . . we need to find a home for our company." Brad Berton, "DreamWorks: Maguire's Nightmare," *Los Angeles Business Journal*, November 18, 1996, p. 1.

41 "Most conventional lenders . . . Playa Vista's project manager. J. William Gibson, "All Wet at Ballona Creek," *L.A. Weekly*, December 6–12, 1996.

42 As writer Jeff Stockwell . . . isn't supposed to win." Jeff Stockwell, "Getting Swamped," *Premiere*, January 1997, p. 52.

42 The trade paper . . . refusing to cooperate with the article. Dan Cox, "Dream Team in Pricey Scheme," *Variety*, September 15, 1997, p. 1.

43 City Councilor Galanter . . . the people's resources for free." Joyzelle Davis, "Studio Shakedown at Playa Vista," *Los Angeles Business Journal*, p. 1.

43 "Jeffrey told me several times . . . we can't afford to do this.'" Galanter interview.

44 "DreamWorks will have no choice . . . another studio or studios to the project." Nick Madigan, "A Dream Built on Sand," *Variety*, August 31, 1998, p. 10.

44 It was Ruth Galanter . . . Make a deal!" Nick Madigan, "DreamWorks Settles on Dream Home," *Variety*, September 28, 1998, p. 18.

44–45 California state senator Tom Hayden . . . uncomfortable to get into a fight with these fellows." J. William Gibson, "Hollywood Sprawl," *The Nation*, March 1, 1999, p. 16.

45 Said Spielberg, "Building our own studio . . . they didn't want to do it after all." Nick Madigan, "Team's Dream Nixed," *Variety*, July 12, 1999, p. 18.

45 In an official statement . . . It was simply not meant to be." Elizabeth Hayes, "Where Now DreamWorks?" *Los Angeles Business Journal*, July 5, 1999, p. 1.

46 "None of the animators would cross the hill . . . outside the city of Los Angeles." Galanter interview.

46 Looking back, Robertson wondered . . . microcosm of the DreamWorks story." Robertson interview.

4: Movies to Go

47 Known as a genuine nice guy . . . what's the big deal." Corliss, "Hey, Let's Put on a Show!" p. 54.

47 "There is no road map . . . It's still evolving." Anita Busch and Rex Weiner, "Gates Joins DreamWorks Team," *Variety*, March 27, 1995, p. 15.

50 It was understood that all three . . . were spread dangerously thin." Josh Young, "Needs Improvement," *Entertainment Weekly*, October 17, 1997, p. 27.

50 Said Katzenberg, "In three years we haven't had an argument, much less a fight." Ibid.

50 Said Geffen, "Jeffrey's become much more user-friendly." Richard Turner and Corie Brown, "Fishing Buddies," *Newsweek*, September 29, 1997, p. 68.

51 There are many ways . . . its first prestige hit. Kim Masters, "Steven Spielberg's Winning Direction: Call 'Tails,'" *Time*, April 7, 1997, p. 22.

53 Charles Taylor . . . as brutal and stupid as men." Charles Taylor, "*The Peacemaker* makes casualties of George Clooney and Nicole Kidman," *Salon*, September 26, 1997.

53 *Variety's* Todd McCarthy . . . grim action thriller." Todd McCarthy, "The Peacemaker (review)," *Variety*, September 22, 1997, p. 37.

55 It was her third novel . . . took up his cause. *Chase-Riboud v. DreamWorks, Inc., et al.*, complaint dated October 17, 1997.

56 Executive producer Walter Parkes . . . against a historical backdrop." Quoted in the complaint, pp. 11–12.

56–57 The author hired Pierce O'Donnell . . . *Coming to America*. Pierce O'Donnell and Dennis McDougal, *Fatal Subtraction* (New York, 1992).

57 "This case is about the original sin . . . for the Jewish Holocaust." Complaint, p. 3.

58 "You can't own a piece of American history," said Fields. "Lawsuits," *Entertainment Weekly*, November 7, 1997, p. 15.

58 He also professed to be surprised . . . grab some money for herself." Bernard Weinraub, "Spielberg Film Faces Charges of Plagiarism," *New York Times*, November 13, 1997, p. E1.

59 "It's amazing . . . efforts on Barbara's credibility." Adam Sandler, "WGA Opens New Chapter in 'Amistad,'" *Variety*, December 8, 1997, p. 2.

60 Chase-Riboud issued a statement . . . having the courage to make it." Dan Cox, "Controversy, Negative Publicity Best Handled Early in Oscar Campaign," *Variety*, March 2, 1998, p. 70.

60 DreamWorks publicity chief . . . awareness of the movie goes up." Ibid.

5: Sideshows

65 David Geffen tried . . . walk away from the ABC deal. "For the DreamWorks Studio, an Unsettling Development," *New York Times*, August 1, 1995, p. D6.

66 "For the last six months . . . wants out of this partnership." Anita M. Busch and Jim Benson, "Troika's Saturday Dreams on Hold," *Variety*, August 7, 1995, p. 17.

67 "Television has been the weakest link in the chain." "Savoring Private Ryan," *U.S. News and World Report*, February 22, 1999, p. 49.

68 "The world has changed . . . new way to be in the TV business. . . ." Michael Schrader, "Company Tunes into TV," *Variety*, August 18, 2003, p. 33.

69 When *Band of Brothers* . . . most expensive television program in history. Jennie L. Phipps, "DreamWorks and HBO Take the High Road with 'Band of Brothers,'" *Electronic Media*, January 7, 2002, p. 26.

70 *Variety* speculated that . . . likeliest home for such a series. Jenny Hontz, "DreamWorks Creates Paramount Pain," *Variety*, June 10, 1996, p. 33.

71 "We started talking about . . . completely different points of view." Interview with Ken Solomon, July 21, 2005.

72 "We realized we had a chance . . . to be a huge success with this thing." Ibid.

72 Chung described . . . an exciting new challenge for me." Bill Carter, "Syndicated Program for Chung and Povich," *New York Times*, June 6, 1996, p. C18.

73 "We figured since we had . . . proved to be right. Solomon interview.

74 "Then we'll get the prime-time access period." Ibid.

75 Several months later Solomon was . . . the old game-show warhorse *Hollywood Squares*. Ibid.

75 "It's not one of our main businesses." Andrew Hinds and Dan Cox, "'Ants' Colony Cranks It Up,'" *Variety*, October 19, 1998, p. 1.

77 "We won't have the baggage . . . a much better success ratio." Gregg Kilda, "In the Works: After One Year Is DreamWorks the Mouse That Roared?" *Entertainment Weekly*, October 20, 1995, p. 38.

77 "I think records could well end up the most valuable part of the company." Andrew E. Serer, "Analyzing the Dream," *Fortune*, April 17, 1995, p. 71.

77 "Mo Ostin is the head . . . I'll help when I can." James Sterngold, "Ex-Head of Warner Records Joins DreamWorks," *New York Times*, October 6, 1995, p. D1.

78 "We're trying to create a haven . . . it will happen again." Josh Young, "Needs Improvement," *Entertainment Weekly*, October 17, 1997, p. 27.

78 "Because of the film's subject . . . that were overtly commercial." Catherine Applefeld Olson, "DreamWorks Hopes to Crown Three 'Princes'," *Billboard*, October 31, 1998, p. 1.

79 "It's part of their lease. We have no recourse." Dan Cox, "Landlord Dethrones 'Prince,'" *Variety*, November 30, 1998, p. 6.

80 In their initial business plan . . . $800 million in feature films. Peter Bart, "The Best Laid Dreams," *Variety*, January 30, 1995, p. 8.

80 "We will release . . . around a dozen titles in 1997." Mark Bernice, "Dream Date," *Broadcasting & Cable*, March 27, 1995, p. 42.

81 "They've got great ideas . . . I don't have the staff." Nick Madigan, "DreamWorks, Free Zone Team for Online Kids Site," *Variety*, COM, November 12, 1997.

81 "DreamWorks hasn't hit . . . a small boutique shop." Sara Fisher, "DreamWorks, Electronic Arts Eyeing Deal," *Los Angeles Business Journal*, January 10, 2000, p. 15.

82 "This is an emerging . . . moment now for the Internet." Rick Lyman, "DreamWorks and Imagine Plan an Internet Venture," *New York Times*, October 26, 1999, p. C10.

82 "Pop's launch is . . . starting to embrace the medium." Mindy Charski, "Picture This: Hollywood in Cyberspace," *Interactive Week*, July 10, 2000, p. 12.

83 "Jeffrey came over and hit a piñata . . . It was kind of kooky." Interview with Tim Doyle, August 20, 2005.

83 "There were times . . . It happened multiple times." Ibid.

84 "The marketing people are loath . . . to innovate and do something interesting." Ibid.

84 "You can't take existing models and port them over to a new-media venture." Richard Tedesco, "Pop.com Goes Bust," *Broadcasting & Cable*, September 11, 2000, p. 17.

6: The Private and the Prince

87 The other two Rs were for *Schindler's List* and *Amistad*, both of which had featured nudity as well as violence.

88 "We're essentially playing guys . . . being made of them constantly." Steven Spielberg and David James, *Saving Private Ryan* (movie tie-in photo book)(New York, 1998).

90 "One of the best things . . . is that Matt Damon became Matt Damon." Andrew Hindes, "Private Ryan's Saving Grace," *Variety*, July 20, 1998, p. 6.

90 "[T]he truth is . . . the world doesn't look quite the same." David Ansen, "Witnessing the Inferno," *Newsweek*, July 27, 1998, p. 57.

90 "quite possibly the greatest combat sequence ever made." Richard Schickel, "Reel War," *Time*, July 27, 1998, p. 56.

90 "the finest war movie of our time." Janet Maslin, "Saving Private Ryan," *New York Times*, July 24, 1998, p. E1.

91 "Hardly a day . . . indicates the depth of its impact." Todd McCarthy, "Pleasant Season of Pix, Mix," *Variety*, August 17, 1998, p. 9.

91 "For ten years I lived . . . on the future of DreamWorks." Anita M. Busch, "Katz Chasing Mouse to Court," *Variety*, April 15, 1996, p. 24.

92 "Katzenberg would have to be . . . and Katzenberg is neither." Anita M. Busch and Adam Sandler, "Disney Returns Fire in War with Katzenberg," *Variety*, May 20, 1996, p. 3.

92 "I wish we didn't feel compelled . . . to protect our turf." Leonard Klady, "DreamWorks Toon 'Prince' Battles Biz's Meanest Season," *Variety*, February 16, 1998, p. 4.

93 "We were about a year and a half . . . Why would Jeffrey do that?" David Hochman, "Epics and Insects," *Newsweek*, November 20, 1998, p. 62.

94 "It was *Mission: Impossible* time. They planned it like the Allies planned Normandy." "Trojan Antz," *Entertainment Weekly*, October 23, 1998, p. 46.

94 Carl Rosendahl . . . a mere "coincidence." Alistair Goldfisher, *Business Journal*, September 14, 1998, p. 1.

94 "No company has yet cracked Disney . . . the war plays out." Todd McCarthy, "Antz (review)," *Variety*, September 21, 1998, p. 104.

95–96 "Every drawing we did was . . . like one of the workers there." Interview with Marc Lumer, July 27, 2005.

96 "He was really working as a moviemaker." Ibid.

96 "Jeffrey was clutching . . . a film that happens to be drawn." Hochman, "Epics and Insects."

97 "Jeffrey's got his publicity machine in place, and that's the source of most of the rumors." Tom Brinkmoeller, "Disney Denies Rumors of Talent Drain from Its Animation Unit to Katzenberg," *Orlando Business Journal*, June 30, 1995, p. 1.

98 Katzenberg claimed dozens of changes . . . that line was a problem." Michael G. Maudlin, "Hollywood on Holy Ground," *Christianity Today*, December 8, 1998, p. 66.

98 "a film that will be more admired than enjoyed." Glenn Lovell, "Prince of Egypt (review)," *Variety*, December 14, 1998, p. 130.

99 "We tried to be uncompromising here . . . to make a camel funny?" Bernard Weinraub, "A Cartoon's Dancing Teapots? Funny Camels? Not for 'Prince of Egypt,'" *New York Times*, December 14, 1998, p. E1.

99 "Jeffrey called us . . . he had made any such call. Hochman, "Epics and Insects."

99–100 Ventrella was quoted in the November 7, 1997, *Entertainment Weekly*, and related the story in private correspondence with the author.

100 "It's an event movie . . . at the end of the year, like 'Titanic.'" Leonard Klady, "D'Works Toon 'Prince' Battles Biz's Meanest Season," *Variety*, February 16, 1998, p. 4.

101 Not counting musicals, the number of comedies that had won to this point could be counted on the fingers of one hand: *It Happened One Night, You Can't Take It with You, The Apartment, The Sting,* and *Annie Hall.*

102 As Peter Biskind recounted . . . planting such rumors. Peter Biskind, *Down and Dirty Pictures* (New York, 2004), p. 369.

103 In fact some surprising articles . . . had been overly praised. Peter Bart, "The Bard's Big Night," *Variety*, March 29, 1999, p. 4.

103 After the ceremonies . . . "Never again!" Biskind, *Down and Dirty Pictures*, p. 371.

7: Open Wide

105 "I am an employee . . . to stick to our tradition." Nick Madigan, "Bigger Dream in the Works," *Variety*, August 2, 1999, p. 7.

105 "We've been fairly vocal . . . on a smaller number of pictures." "Private Spielberg," *Time*, April 5, 1999, p. 64.

106 "What had become fodder . . . would eventually become *American Beauty*." Alan Ball, *American Beauty—The Shooting Script* (New York, 1999), p. 113.

107 "I had seen his production . . . I sort of banked his name in my mind." Bernard Weinraub, "A Wunderkind Discovers the Wonders of Film," *New York Times*, September 12, 1999, p. 120.

107 "It was badly shot . . . It was all my fault." Ibid.

107 "[T]he first few days of . . . he was perfect." Lynn Hirschberg, "Sam Mendes Has Directed Only Two Films . . .," *New York Times*, July 7, 2002, p. E16.

109 "It's a mainstream-but-serious pic . . . thoughtful films have arrived." Charles Lyons, "Early Eyes on the Prize," *Variety*, October 4, 1999, p. 1.

110 "We had a very specific . . . week-by-week basis." Leonard Klady, "The Beauty of Platform Success," *Variety*, October 21, 1999, p. 9.

110–111 "[W]inning awards ups the ante . . . we did with *Saving Private Ryan*." Nick Madigan, "There's No Free Launch," *Variety*, December 13, 1999, p. 56.

111 "You could have called it . . . proud to accept it." Dave McNary, "Helmers Hail Mendes for his 'Beauty' Mark," *Variety*, March 20, 2000, p. 10.

112 Bening and Swank would face off again in 2004, and Swank would win again, this time for *Million Dollar Baby*.

112 "Most [studio distribution] vets agree . . . should serve as a textbook case." Dade Hayes, "Beauty B.O. Gets Oscar Uplift," *Variety*, April 3, 2000, p. 13.

8: In the Arena

115–116 "When we were doing *El Dorado*. . . the perception that they copied the other." Lumer interview.

116 "Because this was a broader-appeal movie . . . these kinds of alliances." T. L. Stanley, "Road Show," *Brandweek*, January 24, 2000, p. 4.

119 "I can do that." Diana Landau, ed., *Gladiator: The Making of the Ridley Scott Epic* (New York, 2000), p. 11.

121 The only American notably doing similar work was Will Vinton, who concentrated on shorts, TV shows like *The PJs*, and advertising, most famously the California Raisins.

121 As with *El Dorado*, DreamWorks . . . Chevron, Clorox, and Kroger supermarkets. Wayne Friedman, "'Chicken' plucks $100 Mil for Media, Marketing Run," *Advertising Age*, June 19, 2000, p. 3.

122 "As DreamWorks has matured . . . just building the company." Paul F. Duke, "Dream Duo Reups with Production on Plate," *Variety*, May 29, 2000, p. 12.

122 "Hollywood is finally taking note: DreamWorks has truly arrived." Paul F. Duke, "D'Works: What Lies Beneath?" *Variety*, July 24, 2000, p. 1.

122 "DreamWorks is teaching . . . no demographic stone unturned." "Season's Gradings," *Entertainment Weekly*, September 8, 2000, p. 10.

123 "It's a dysfunctional studio . . . that works very well." Paul F. Duke, "D'Works: What Lies Beneath?", p. 1.

124 "We are hurt and despondent . . . at the wrong time." Rick Lyman, "Slump Vexes Creators of 'Almost Famous,'" *New York Times*, October 19, 2000, p. E3.

125–126 The author is a member and past president of the group.

9: Easy Being Green

130 "The story itself was . . . the sensibility of the movie." John Hopkins, *Shrek: From the Swamp to the Screen* (New York, 2004), p. 15.

130–131 "I don't think Mike understood . . . now we had gold." Steve Daly, "Green Party: Color Him Impressive!", *Entertainment Weekly*, May 25, 2001, p. 44.

132 "*Shrek* has a very subversive attitude . . . We take shots at everybody." Video excerpts from the 2001 *Shrek* press conference at Cannes are available online at *http://www.festival-cannes .fr/films/fiche_film.php?langue=6002&partie=video&id_film= 1100045&cmedia=3937*.

132–133 "In this version of things . . . at its animation rival, Disney." "A Shrek of a Summer," *Newsweek*, May 7, 2001, p. 62.

133 "an instant animated classic." Todd McCarthy, "*Shrek* Will Charm Kids, Adults on Road to Cannes," *Variety*, May 7, 2001, p. 49.

133 "This charmingly loopy, iconoclastic story . . . such skill and chutzpah." Lisa Schwarzbaum, "Forest Grump: DreamWorks Takes Playful Aim at Some Mouse House Icons in Its Delightful New Animated Feature Shrek," *Entertainment Weekly*, May 25, 2001, p. 50.

135 "To be sure, DreamWorks still . . . remains a pure film play." Peter Bart, "Hits Aside, How Will the Dream Work?" *Variety*, April 2, 2001, p. 1.

137 The film had no direct connection . . . "arrives at a tricky moment," according to one review. Todd McCarthy, "Stars Hot, But Will Auds Go for Jailbait?", *Variety*, October 23, 2001, p. 33.

139 "If the nominations go to . . . the British Academy of Film & Television Arts (BAFTA). "Eddie Murphy: Oscar Nominee?", *Business Week Online*, February 1, 2002.

139 "We're putting everything behind *Monsters*. . . . it's the best toon prize." Paul Karon, "Beastly Battle Brewing," *Variety*, December 24, 2001, p. 33.

140 DreamWorks took out an ad . . . paying homage to another giant of the animation field. "Chuck Jones 1912–2002" (ad), *Variety*, March 11, 2002, p. 15.

140–141 "DreamWorks Pictures would like . . . the very first Oscar for Best Animated Film." "Thanks" (ad), *Variety*, April 1, 2002, p. 2–3.

10: Follow the Money

142–143 "The reason the American . . . producers hold all the rights." Rex Weiner, "DreamWorks Taking a Rights Turn," *Variety*, May 8, 1995, p. 27.

143 Chemical Banking Corp. . . . credit line for DreamWorks. Daniel Dunaief, "Chemical Wins Starring Role in $1B Loan to Spielberg & Co.'s Multimedia Venture," *American Banker*, March 31, 1995, p. 1.

144 "With a huge database . . . from video rentals." "*Shrek* and *Friends* Unlock Value for DreamWorks," *Structured Finance International*, September–October 2002, p. 42.

144 For a discussion of the origin of the term "monkey points," see O'Donnell and McDougal, *Fatal Subtraction*, p. 200.

145 "If you wonder why a studio . . . might be considered a flop." Renee Harmon, *The Beginning Filmmaker's Business Guide* (New York, 1994), p. 79.

146 An analysis of the Spielberg/Cruise 2002 hit film . . . realized less than $20 million apiece. Laura M. Holson, "So, What's the Spielberg Magic Worth?" *New York Times*, November 28, 2005, p. C1.

147 "It's a lot of money if you only have a handful of pictures to release in a year." Beth Laski and Leonard Klady, "Next for 'Works: Domestic Distrib'n," *Variety*, June 19, 1995, p. 11.

149 "The initial theatrical release . . . than an outside distributor would be." Geraldine Fabrikant, "MCA to Distribute Dream-Works's Films Abroad," *New York Times*, June 14, 1995, p. D9.

11: Catch as Catch Can

153 "Today, we have technologies . . . which is exciting." *The Time Machine*, studio press kit, p. 2.

154 "In just five years . . . launch successful pics." Dade Hayes, "Festival Forays Pay Off for DreamWorks," *Variety*, May 13, 2002, p. 35.

155 "We had to do a first . . . to be metaphorical, not descriptive. *Spirit: Stallion of the Cimarron* press conference, Cannes Film Festival, excerpts at *http://www.festival-cannes.fr/films/fiche_film .php?langue=6002&partie=video&id_film=3016607&cmedia= 4459.*

156 To help animators understand . . . *Spirit: Die Horse*. Film critic Ed Symkus interviewed Jeffrey Katzenberg before the release of *Spirit* and provided a transcript of the interview to the author.

156 "Horses are among the most . . . no animal more difficult to animate." *Spirit: Stallion of the Cimarron* press kit, p. 3.

156 "I think we're going to see . . . the creative styles." Barbara Robertson, "Free Spirits," *Computer Graphics World*, May 2002, p. 22.

157–158 "I still look at *Spirit* . . . just be spellbound by it." Interview with Jeffrey Katzenberg by Ed Symkus, March 2006.

158 "If our movies were coming out . . . the moviegoers look forward to these films." Interview with Jeffrey Katzenberg by Ed Symkus, May 2002.

158–159 "DreamWorks keeps making its own rules. . . taps into disparate creative energies." Dade Harris, "So How DOES the Dream Work?", *Variety*, June 10, 2002, p. 1.

159 "I am impressed by their numbers . . . We feel the need to push boundaries." Ibid.

161 "That is the core of the story . . . what can be more important than that?" *Road to Perdition* press kit, p. 19.

161 "With *Perdition* there are two layers . . . a more conventional narrative about fathers and sons." Hirschberg, "Sam Mendes Has Directed Only Two Films . . .," p. E16.

162 "Look at how many movies are out . . . July and August benefited the movie." Pete Hammond, "Early Entries Can Be Awards Curse," *Variety*, December 23, 2002, p. 37.

165 "Mark said, 'I've just seen the scariest movie . . . we were going to remake the movie." *The Ring* press kit, p. 2.

167 "It was a good solid year. 'The Ring' left everyone on a big high." Marc Graser, "D'Works Rings in Transitional Note for 2003," *Variety*, Yearbook supplement, January 20, 2003, p. A-9.

12: Taking Stock

169 Excluding films partnered with other studios that were released by those studios.

170 "our attempt to do an homage to . . . *Indiana Jones* in animation." Katzenberg interview with Ed Symkus, May 2002.

170 "We are extremely disappointed . . . traditional animation is likely a thing of the past." Laura M. Holson, "Animated Title Is Latest Film to Run Aground at DreamWorks," *New York Times*, July 21, 2003, p. C1.

171 "This is our first shitty year." Kim Master, "What's Wrong with DreamWorks?", *Esquire*, November 2003, p. 94.

172 "This is a transitional year for us . . . your development always suffers." Marc Graser, "Needed: A New Shark Trek," *Variety*, August 18, 2003, p. 1.

172 "Studios can overreact . . . not the other way around." Ibid.

172 "It's not difficult to manage . . . one filled with big-budget failures." Master, "What's Wrong with DreamWorks?", p. 94.

173 "The films emerging from DreamWorks . . . there are fewer of them." Peter Bart, "The Strivings of Sir Steven," *Daily Variety*, Gotham Edition, July 19, 2004, p. 4.

173–174 "The greatest contribution I've made . . . if they're not Walter's projects." Master, "What's Wrong with DreamWorks?", p. 94.

174 "I want them to be comfortable and happy." Peter Kafka, "Married to the Job," *Forbes*, March 3, 2003, p. 86.

175 "counting on a blockbuster *Shrek 2*. . . its animation unit later this year." Ronald Grover, "DreamWorks' IPO Prequel?", *Business Week*, May 24, 2004, p. 13.

175 "I felt we had only told part of the story. I felt it was incomplete." Hopkins, *Shrek: From the Swamp to the Screen*, p. 52.

176 "We thought we would get in the 70s . . . playing exceptionally at every level." Dave McNary, "B.O. Ogre-Achiever: $104 Mil," *Daily Variety*, Gotham Edition, May 24, 2004, p. 1.

177 "I love making animation movies . . . Who can explain why? It's chemistry." Harry Haun, "Shrek, Sharks, & Beyond," *Film Journal International*, July 2004, p. 52.

179 "The average domestic box office . . . do not intend to produce any such films." DreamWorks Animation prospectus, October 27, 2004, p. 1.

179 This was intended . . . to "make us a less attractive takeover target." Prospectus, p. 25.

179 Spielberg decided to decline . . . compensation for directing films at DreamWorks. Ronald Grover, "DreamWorks' IPO, Disney's Nightmare," *Business Week Online*, July 22, 2004.

13: Merge Ahead

181 "This past October, DreamWorks celebrated . . . embark on the next 10 years." Letter with 2005 Preview Kit, December 2004.

182 "It's no secret that we have wanted . . . the reins of the day-to-day running of the studio." Thomas Gale, "Dream Team Takes Flight," *Daily Variety*, May 18, 2005, p. 1.

183 "This was the man who literally created . . . series of novels by Japanese horror writer Koji Suzuki. *The Ring 2* press kit, p. 3.

184 "When you talk up a film the way they did, you'd better deliver." Ronald Grover, "How DreamWorks Lost (Wall) Street Cred," *Business Week*, June 20, 2005, p. 48.

185 "I think it would be imprudent to come to a conclusion about this yet." Merissa Marr, "In DreamWorks Earning Woes, a Bigger Problem," *Wall Street Journal*, July 12, 2005, p. A1.

185–186 "We still want to make important movies, but I do believe the palette is broadening." Nicole LaPorte, "Dream Machine Gets a Facelift," *Variety*, July 11, 2005, p. 1.

186 "It's pretty funny—he was watching all my dailies. *Spielberg* watching your dailies!" Ibid.

186–187 "Adam Goodman has been an integral part . . . his capability to lead that team." Nicole LaPorte, "D'Works Locks in Players," *Daily Variety*, August 8, 2005, p. 1.

187 "The biggest mistake this company made was we made a date, not a movie." Nicole LaPorte, "Sinking 'Island': The Ripple Effect," *Variety*, August 1, 2005, p. 6.

189 "We pursued it for quite some time . . . and we're no longer in discussions with them." Kate Kelly and Bruce Orwall, "DreamWorks Ends Talks with Universal," *Wall Street Journal*, September 27, 2005, p. A3.

190 "You can't believe how upset that made David . . . He thought he had a deal." Ronald Grover, "Memo to GE: Don't Cross David Geffen," *Business Week Online*, December 13, 2005.

191 "The value for Paramount was irrefutable . . . to get the deal done." Merissa Marr, Kate Kelly, and Kathryn Kranhold, "Hollywood Rewrite: Viacom Outbids GE to Buy DreamWorks," *Wall Street Journal*, December 12, 2005, p. 1.

191 "I was saddened that . . . with Universal's parent company, GE." Ibid.

192 "There are only three real brand names in the movie business—Spielberg, Pixar and Miramax—and Spielberg is number one." "End of the Dream," *The Economist*, December 17, 2005, p. 63.

192 Paramount eased its costs . . . making the company seem like a bargain. "Viacom to Sell Paramount Pictures' DreamWorks Film Library for $900 Million," Viacom press release, March 17, 2006.

Epilogue: Why Did DreamWorks Fail?

194 Allen's share of the Paramount sale, according to Geffen, was "profit for him." Jill Goldsmith, "It 'Works for Par," *Daily Variety*, December 12, 2005, p. 1.

196 "We started DreamWorks because . . . We're dealing with our own." Geraldine Fabrikant with Rick Lyman, "Dreaming in Tighter Focus," *New York Times*, September 25, 2000, p. C1.

196 "Our eyes were bigger than our stomachs . . . a great deal in ten years." Laura M. Holson and Sharon Waxman, "Despite Success of 'Shrek,' DreamWorks Has Work to Do to Woo Wall Street," *New York Times*, May 17, 2004, p. C8.

198 "DreamWorks is . . . Those days are way over." Kim Masters, "The Best Little Movie Studio in Hollywood," *Esquire*, September 2001, p. 88.

199 Bob Bennett, who worked for John Kluge . . . was bought by Murdoch for $65 million. Daniel M. Kimmel, *The Fourth Network* (Chicago, 2004), p. 10.

200–201 "Lew will take on a lot of very important . . . marketing of our movies and the movies themselves," Merissa Marr, "DreamWorks Fills a New Post in Move to Sharpen CEO's Focus," *Wall Street Journal*, December 6, 2005, p. B6.

202 "If they weren't as good . . . couldn't have been a co-studio head and a director." Masters, "What's Wrong with DreamWorks?", p. 94.

202 "Walter is in a giant, giant conflict-of-interest . . . getting paid as a producer." Ibid.

204–206 "If you see anything in the movie that's not done . . . Never say, 'Never again.'" The quotes from Tim Johnson and Jeffrey Katzenberg are from their presentation at the AMC Boston Common Theaters private screening of *Over the Hedge*, March 27, 2006.

Index

A NOTE ON THE AUTHOR

Daniel M. Kimmel is the Boston correspondent for *Variety* and has written for numerous publications, including the *Boston Globe*, the *Christian Science Monitor*, *Film Comment*, and the *Worcester* (Massachusetts) *Telegram and Gazette*, where he reviews films. He also writes a column on classic science-fiction films for the *Internet Review of Science Fiction*. Born on Long Island, New York, he studied at the University of Rochester and received a law degree from Boston University. Mr. Kimmel has taught film and media-related courses at Emerson College, Boston University, and Suffolk University. His book *The Fourth Network*, about FOX television, won the Cable Center Book Award. He is also co-author of *The Waldorf Conference*, about the birth of the Hollywood blacklist, and of *Love Stories*, a book of essays about Hollywood's most romantic movies. He lives in Brookline, Massachusetts, with his wife and daughter.